ELEVATE YOUR VOICE

Courageous Stories to Inspire Strength, Perseverance, and Hope

A LIGHTbeamers book by April Adams Pertuis
in collaboration with the following authors
(in alphabetical order):

Julia Barton

Becky Burroughs

Kristy Castilleja

Dr. Brittany Clayborne

Tessa Kidd

Marie Masse

Pamela Meadows

Sheryl Morley

Penny Pereboom

Leanne Smith

Deb Cummins Stellato

Stephanie Talia

Kofi Williams

Library of Congress Control Number: 2022902240
ISBN: 978-1-7327858-2-3

Positivity Lady Press
Robbinston, ME 04671
www.positivityladypress.com

This anthology is a work of creative non-fiction. All of the events depicted are true to the best of the author's memory. Some names and identifying features have been changed to protect the identity of certain parties. The author in no way represents the views of any company, corporation, or brand. Views expressed are solely those of each author.

This book is dedicated to the members of the LIGHTbeamers Community who have shown up to bravely share their stories. Although fourteen specific stories are told in this book, we share them to honor and encourage all of you.

Table of Contents

INTRODUCTION

I was nine years old when I first learned it was risky for women to speak up and use their voices.

I was boarding the bus after school when the bus driver told me my house was no longer on his route. Turns out, my mom had spoken up at a recent school board meeting about a matter she thought was important and worth fighting for, but the only thing she accomplished was getting me kicked off the bus and left trying to figure out how I was going to get home.

Women have long been fighting battles like that one. We find the courage and gumption to speak up, only to get our hands slapped, our name tarnished, or, worst of all, our souls crushed—sending us back where we came from: a place where we play small, keep quiet, and go along with things to keep the peace.

Even though my bus incident took place more than forty years ago, there is still a lot of work to do. I encounter women every single day who have spent the last forty years cramming themselves into a small box and trying their best to fit an ideal that was built by someone else's ego, trauma, or power trip.

As women, we go along for the ride. Willingly. Not knowing the long-term damage it causes.

We've lost ourselves, ladies!

For the past several years, I've sat with women while they poured out the puzzle pieces of their stories and began the healing process of sorting them and putting them back together. When they begin, their story is in shambles. In most cases, they feel inadequate—utterly unworthy of the time and energy needed to sort through the rubble. They come to the table shouldering the "should'ves" and shame that life has piled onto them. They look at the ransacked pieces of their life and wonder, What in the hell does it all mean, anyway? What's the point of all this?

Too many women stop there. They see their puzzle pieces as messes they can't clean up.

In our work together, we look for the perimeter pieces first—the ones that are easy to spot with their straight edges and corners that easily build a frame in which the rest of their puzzle pieces live.

Then, one by one, we find interior pieces that go together: all of the beautiful pinks that make up the gorgeous bouquet, or the smiles that fit together to remind them of the people in their lives who matter most.

Slowly . . . these women come back to themselves.

The last few pieces that fall into place are the ones that anchor them and connect them to all the other pieces of their story.

And then a woman remembers.

She remembers who she is. She rediscovers her inner fire. She is reignited with her passion, and a light emerges.

Women don't need to spend one more minute carrying the junk from past stories and old wounds when we can be using our stories in much more powerful ways.

Women don't need to be reminded of our place; we need to claim our place.

At the beginning of 2021, I heard a specific call from God. I was in a period of asking and praying for guidance as I embarked on the new year—and I asked, "What do I need to do next? How can I serve others in the highest way that will honor you?"

He answered: Elevate women's voices.

I had no idea that meant writing a book—but it turns out, that was a piece of my own puzzle that fit perfectly once some of the other pieces were put together.

As it often does, the Spirit moved quickly, and before the end of the year, fourteen women had come together to share their stories for this compilation book. No other title was even considered besides Elevate Your Voice.

For that's exactly what the authors you'll meet here are doing. They are stepping out of their own small boxes and stretching themselves out of the years they've spent adhering to what others think and say.

It will forever be risky for women to use their voices if we don't start using them.

Although many other brave women have gone before us and made serious headway, making it possible for fourteen women to write and publish a book—freely and without the need for permission—there is still a lot at stake.

Each of these women submitted her story with hefty doses of trepidation: What will other people think? What will my boss say? What if my words are taken out of context? What if my message doesn't land? What if nobody reads it? What if my writing isn't any good?

Maybe you've had a dream on your heart for some time of pouring out your own story puzzle, but fear has stepped in and intervened. Maybe some of those same thoughts have crossed your mind.

We write these stories for you.

I hope you'll see yourself in one or two of the stories in this book, and that in some way, it leads you back to your own puzzle and you find the piece you've been missing.

Now more than ever, we need women like you to speak up and share their stories. Our daughters, and those who will come behind them, need us to keep elevating our voices. . . . And make them louder and louder and louder.

I hope this book and the stories inside reach an audible level no one can ignore.

Listen. Do you hear it?

This is for the feminine collective, and we are here to elevate our voices. Will you join us?

Say yes! We have a seat for you at our table.

Cheering for you,
April

Chapter 1

STAND UP FOR YOURSELF

April Adams Pertuis

"It was about discovering my true value, and in finding that, I found my voice."

There have been a whole bunch of Sams in my career. I call them Sams, named after the original Sam who entered my life while I was making my way through journalism school. Sam was a student in the broadcasting program where I was enrolled. I'm not even sure how we first became friends. I just remember him being a likable guy. He was outgoing and good-looking, and others seemed to like him as well.

Sam befriended me. We were both go-getters and eager to perform at the top of our class. He complimented me and encouraged me as we dove deep into broadcasting projects like news gathering, video production, and editing. But as time went on, Sam's dark side showed up. If I was chosen to direct the team or to take the spotlight, Sam's claws came out. He'd try to undermine my decisions in an attempt to make me question my ideas. Or he'd give (un)constructive criticism in the guise of trying to help me be better.

After a few months of this, I grew tired of Sam. He frustrated me. I struggled to find ways to respond to his remarks without fueling his fire. He had a smooth way of turning the tables on me and making me feel small and helpless. I felt impeded. Silenced. Voiceless. When I looked at him, all I could see was an insurmountable roadblock in my way. No matter which direction I chose, he'd show up, and I'd have to figure out how to navigate around him. He became an omnipresent figure in my day. I dreaded walking into the journalism department (a place I had once loved) because I knew he'd be there. The worst was when we were alone, working extra hours on a project; his aggression was always on display when others weren't around to witness it.

I had never met a guy like Sam before. He was manipulative, undermining, and smooth. He threw me off my game, leaving me feeling incapable in many ways. Some days, I'd end up utterly despondent and broken, curled up in tears in my dorm room after class.

Finally, I'd had enough. I realized it was either Sam or my career . . . and no way in hell was I choosing Sam. I had a really great relationship with the two department heads—two men I greatly respected and admired. Nervously, I went to them and asked for help. I explained how Sam was causing me stress with his bullying tactics and aggression. I felt disempowered when he was around. I needed someone to intervene. I hadn't learned how to deal with a narcissist in my life yet. I was twenty-three. Sam was my training ground.

Things turned ugly.

Sam was approached about my complaints, and boy oh boy, did he want to make me pay.

It all came to a head one day when a bunch of students, including Sam and me, were sitting outside the studio after class. Our professors were handing out assignments, delegating roles in the next newscast we were to produce for the school. I was assigned a leading role, and Sam was assigned to a supporting role on my team. Almost simultaneously, we both protested. Sam couldn't stand the thought of me leading him, and I couldn't bear another minute of his vitriol as my teammate.

An argument between the two of us erupted in front of our classmates and our professors. Sam took every complaint of mine and twisted and turned it around like a pretzel and pointed all blame back on me.

Basically, it was all my fault he was an asshole.

One of the department heads stepped in. He pointed at Sam and told him he was out of line. He could either accept the role and work with me in compliance or remove himself from the show altogether. Sam chose the latter.

By now, I was sick to my stomach. I knew he wasn't going away that easily.

After we'd been dismissed, I left the building. Sam followed me. From behind, I could hear him calling out my name. "April, stop! Come back here. I want to talk to you!"

I ignored him and kept walking to my car.

His commands got louder and more demanding: "Stop right now. Listen to me!"

No I won't, Sam. I'm done with you! I thought, and I kept walking until I got to my car.

Sam was fast. Before I could open my door all the way, he was there slamming it shut, pinning me between him and the car.

In my face, he yelled at me. *"I said I want to talk to you*!"

"I don't want to talk to you, Sam. I said what I had to say back there in the studio. I'm done."

I tried to remain calm, but I could feel myself slipping. My neck was turning red, and I could feel my throat closing up. The burning feeling of tears hinted on the backside of my eyes.

I wanted to shove him out of my way, but Sam towered over me. He was not a small man. He was burly, strong, and physical. His face was red with anger.

At that moment, I was *done* giving all my power away to him. I'd spent months in utter anguish over his tirades, snide remarks, and criticism that came in the guise of trying to make me a better journalist. Time and time again, I'd go home at the end of class feeling defeated and voiceless. Sam's remarks would sting, and they made me question my ability to direct and lead a team. If I couldn't manage Sam, how was I going to lead production teams in the future? I had lost sleep, my appetite, and many tears over his presence in my life.

I had no more energy for him.

Standing in the parking lot, with Sam's hand on my door preventing me from leaving, I looked him directly in the eyes and said, "Sam, get your hand off my door. You either get away from me right now, or I'm going back into the studio to report you. This ends today. I am not your friend. We are done here."

Despite my best attempt to stay calm and exude confidence in that moment, I was shaking.

I wanted to throw up.

This man literally made me sick to my stomach.

I couldn't believe I was under this much stress over a guy with whom I had absolutely no connection other than the fact that we both happened to be at the same school, taking the same classes, trying to get a degree in the same field. We both wanted to be journalists.

For some reason, I was a threat to him. It was like there was only ever going to be *one job* available for both of us, and he was putting us through some sort of a Darwinian fight to see who was going to come out on top.

He exerted his power over me to make himself feel better. And he probably succeeded, because I know for sure I always felt worse after being around him.

Sam stared at me. I stared back at him, refusing to look away. I could feel myself slipping; I was forcing back tears while silently willing him away with every ounce of energy in my body.

He removed his hand from my door, and I got in my car and drove away. I never spoke to him again.

It's been over twenty-five years, and I've never forgotten him.

Unfortunately, there were many more Sams to come in my career.

That was just a warm-up.

At my last job in broadcasting, I worked as a weekday news reporter and weekend anchor at a CBS affiliate in Arkansas. I was up for a promotion to a full-time weekday anchor position. After a series of conversations, the general manager of the station offered me the job. I had spent the last twenty-four hours deliberating about the job description, expectations, and, most importantly, *the pay*.

I was married by then, and my husband is the perfect blend of wise advice and compassionate listening. He had been coaching me and helping me prepare for my meeting with the GM, presumably to accept the offer.

The problem was that the promotion didn't come with a pay raise. I was being promoted in title only. And, if you want to get to the real nitty-gritty, the hours were *worse*. The weekday morning anchor gets up around 3:00 a.m. to be on the desk for the morning show each day. It wasn't necessarily my dream job, but I was eager to get a full-time anchor position. It was the leg up I needed to advance my career.

I decided the early morning hours were something I could get used to, but what I couldn't swallow was the fact that I was being offered the promotion without a pay increase.

Sitting in the office with the general manager, I inquired why this was.

I must have drunk an extra cup of coffee with a spoonful of courage that morning, because I boldly asked, "Is this pay rate the same as the gentleman's I will be replacing?"

I did not get an answer to that question. Instead, the GM implied that the promotion and title should be enough for me. I should be grateful for the opportunity.

"This is a great move for you, April. This is an opportunity most of your colleagues are begging for."

Boom. There it was. The story line women have been fed all of our lives.

We should be grateful for the opportunities that come our way, for they could have just as easily been given to someone else. Or someone more agreeable!

We should be grateful someone is giving us the attention and fancy title.

We should be grateful for the job to begin with. Don't get ahead of yourself. Don't ask for more!

Just like when Sam had tried all those years earlier to help me be a "better" journalist, when I should have been grateful for his hurtful words and bullying ways.

I realized the pattern had been repeating itself. Sam used manipulation and aggression. The GM leaned on the culture of the male patriarchy in the news business. Either way, I felt oppressed.

I was disgusted and pissed. I knew I was ready and qualified for this job, and I wanted a pay raise.

I calmly looked up at the GM and slid the paperwork he was expecting me to sign back across the desk to him.

"I'm afraid I'll have to pass. If the job doesn't come with a raise, then I'll stay where I am in my current role."

I literally wanted to jump out of my chair and give myself a high five. I had delivered that line just as my husband and I had rehearsed it!

The general manager looked puzzled and shocked. "I'm really sorry to hear that, April. I felt certain we would walk out of here today with a deal."

"No deal, but thank you. I really appreciate it." (I had to add the thank-you and the appreciation, because I should be grateful, right?)

Within three months of that conversation, I made the decision to leave television news. It was a soul-sucking job, and the benefits and rewards simply weren't there. It was a rat race, and I didn't want to be a rat.

At this point in my life, something was stirring inside of me. A restlessness and a deep knowing that I had been made for more. Many people thought I was nuts for leaving such a high-profile and promising career . . . but deep down I was seeking something I couldn't find in the corporate setting: autonomy. I was curious what it would be like to create a path for myself that was fully my own.

The oppression bled throughout my young career like a bad rash I couldn't get rid of. I was agitated but didn't have a real vision yet how to cure it. Instinctively, I sensed that the only way to overcome the oppression was to be smarter than the oppressor.

I left my career behind to begin this new quest: to forge my own way, on my own terms, designing a future that would allow me to step more powerfully into a life I designed.

It was a huge shock to people when they learned I had left my job without a new job lined up! They assumed I was leaving because I had landed a better job in a larger market with a higher-profile position as anchor. It was hard for them to understand, but not once did I question my decision. It was one of the best decisions I ever made. It set me on a path to discovering who I am as a journalist and storyteller. Turns out, I am grateful to the GM. He presented me with a golden opportunity to discover what it feels like to exercise my voice. Sam had done that for me too, that day in the parking lot.

Both times I was nervous and shaky. My neck turned red, and my throat felt like it would close up completely, leaving me unable to breathe or swallow. However, a seed was planted in me. Those challenging situations were merely opportunities for me to exercise my voice, to claim my worth, and to stand firm in my power. My voice was in there somewhere, exercised in ways I didn't know I had in me, and the taste of it left me wanting more!

Believe me when I say it was *hard* to muster up the courage to face those two men and the many other Sams I've encountered in my career. They all came wearing different disguises, but their agenda was always the same: to exert power over me and to keep me quiet and in my place.

For more years than I care to admit, I dealt with this ongoing subtle abuse. It's sneaky. If you don't have your antennae on high alert, you'll miss it, and it will seep in without your permission.

I'd love to tell you that I got really good at defusing the Sams . . . but the truth is, I didn't. They kept showing up in my life because I hadn't quite figured out how to stop them. As they say, God will keep sending you the teacher until you learn the lesson.

It wasn't until many years later, when I made a big cross-country move, that I finally started listening to

God and trusting myself at a whole new level. I often joke that I had to move back to Texas to find my Texas-sized big girl panties.

On a practical level, we moved to be closer to family. My dad was in very poor health, and it was important to be closer to home to help with his needs.

On a spiritual level, I had to move to Texas to find my space.

Just a few years before our move, I had started writing and sharing my stories on social media. At first they were pretty neutral and innocent. They were full of encouragement and inspiration, but honestly, they were pretty vanilla and benign. I had also started a private community, and up until our move, the community had been pretty quiet. I created the space to invite women to share their stories, but I hadn't exactly figured out how to get them to show up and be bold with their voices.

I realize now it had to do with the fact that I was still trying to figure that out for myself!

Moving conjured up all sorts of feelings for me. It was a very emotional time, and the ground underneath me felt like quicksand. I had spent the previous eighteen years planting roots and investing in a home I loved, a community I loved, a city I loved, a church I loved, and friends I loved.

In Texas, I felt untethered.

Who were my people? Where was my community? What did I have to offer here? I felt like an outsider looking in. There was no sense of belonging for me.

So here I was—in a new home, in a new city, with no friends, no church, no coworkers (by now, I was running my own business and working from home), and no connection to tie me down and ground me. Yes, I had family here, but even that felt new to me, because we had spent nearly twenty years apart.

I turned to the only place I felt any sense of control and connection—the community I had built online called LIGHTbeamers. I deeply desired conversation and stimulation, so I began delivering prompts and storytelling challenges in an effort to get more members involved and showing up with their stories. I was starved for friendships and community, so I poured myself into this group. It was the only place I could find what I was looking for. I began to share my story, exposing vulnerable sides of myself that felt too big to hold inside anymore. Big cross-country moves are hard . . . and I was openly sharing my "hard" with them. This felt like therapy to me.

There were real, authentic moments, from sharing my heartbreak over moving to concerns around my dad's health. My emotions were just under the surface, and that surface was thin and fragile. I was on edge and riding the roller coaster day after day. One minute I was sad, the next minute I was angry. I covered most of it up with a smile and continued to throw myself into my work because it was the only thing that made me feel sane and in control.

Finally, about a year after our move, we began to look for a church. We had left behind an amazing church community, and it was important to find a place where our family could worship and meet new people. Our kids were also navigating their own emotions from the move, so we were looking for a youth group where they could dig in and connect with kids their age.

After hopping around for months to different churches, we finally settled on one that felt like a good fit for our family. We found ourselves getting connected, meeting new people, and really enjoying the Sunday sermons. The pastor seemed like a great guy, and he'd gone out of his way to make us feel welcomed as newcomers.

One Sunday after church, the pastor held an information session on the life of the church. All newcomers were invited to learn more about its mission and vision. The goal was to help us make an informed decision about whether we were ready to explore church membership.

My husband had a prior commitment, so I attended the meeting solo.

At first, it seemed everything the pastor was saying checked off all of our boxes.

- Theology
- Mission
- Giving
- Youth
- Community

But then he got to organizational development.

You see, this was a brand-new church, recently planted, without a lot of the constructs most churches have once they become established. There were no elders or deacons in place yet.

In Presbyterian churches, elders and deacons serve as leaders of the church, helping govern and make important decisions about the life of the congregation. I had served as a deacon at our previous church for three years. It was one of the most challenging and rewarding experiences of my life. Talk about service— church leadership is one where you literally have to remove yourself and think of others first. It was one of the most humbling experiences I'd ever been a part of, and I loved every minute of it!

The pastor explained that this new church was part of the Presbyterian Church in America (PCA). Our previous church was Presbyterian Church USA (PCUSA). I wasn't aware of the difference between the two denominations except that one was considered moderate and the other was a little more conservative.

Then, the pastor informed us that once this new church grew big enough to ordain elders and deacons, those roles would go only to the men.

INSERT HARD STOP.

Say what???

The leadership of this brand-new church, planted in the twenty-first century, will be handled only by the men?

Did I hear that correctly?

I asked a slew of probing questions, because surely I had misunderstood what he was saying.

Nope. This church and the doctrine of the PCA points toward men being the only ones God calls into office. This is not the case in the PCUSA; they have been ordaining women for decades.

Suddenly, I couldn't breathe. I could feel that old familiar feeling of my neck turning red and my throat closing up. I had to get out of there.

As soon as the meeting was adjourned, I said my polite goodbyes and thank-yous and made a quick escape. In the car, I burst into tears. Sobbing, I had to keep wiping my eyes so that I could see the road in front of me.

I was so distraught because I had just moved my family across the country into the land of back-ass thinking and belief systems. I had just given up the home I loved, the people I loved, the community I loved, and the church I loved—*for what?* All of the emotions I had been bottling up since this big move exploded like a firecracker. I was utterly overcome in that moment.

The very fact that my family had felt so at home at this church and felt called to become repeat visitors, and even give membership serious consideration, made me question *everything.*

Was I just nuts? Had I completely lost it?

Ever since stepping out on my own after leaving the news business all those years ago, I had forged my way in the world using my own skills and talents. And although I had encountered more Sams along the way, I hadn't hit roadblocks that denied me access simply because I was a woman. Sure, I'd felt slighted here and there, but nothing to this degree. In my mind, this took oppression to a whole new level.

This was all God's fault. I had heard His voice in the dead of night calling me home to Texas, and this is where He'd sent me?

"I don't know anyone here other than my sister," I cried out loud in the car, angry with God and His direction. "My dad's health is getting worse. I have no friends and no sense of community here . . . and the minute I start to feel comfy in this community of faith, you drop this hammer on me?"

There will be no women leaders of this church.

Because we women should be grateful, right? Grateful that God has ordained the men to be leaders, and left the easier roles up to us.

It's like all the Sams I'd ever encountered in my life were piled in the car with me like circus clowns with terrible merry-go-round music playing in the background, laughing at me and piercing me with their glee.

Take that, April.

All of my anger and frustration exploded to the top.

I called my husband on the way home. He couldn't make out a word I was saying as I heaved and sobbed and sputtered out things like, "I can't believe this" and "What the fuck?"

Thankfully, my husband has been there since the very first Sam experience, and he's watched my plight as a woman and become my most valued and treasured ally in the fight. Like he always does, he reassured me and did his best to calm me down. He reassured me that I wasn't crazy, and validated my feelings with his own statements like, "Of course women should be allowed into office. Anything less than that is antiquated and true lack-thinking."

Despite my husband's reassurances, I fell asleep that night doubting and questioning everything. I felt despondent, not just because of what I had learned at the church meeting, but because all the stories of women I had interviewed and worked with over the years flooded into my head and played on a continuous loop.

A few days later, the pastor emailed me inviting me to coffee. He's a smart guy. He'd noted my battery of questions at the information meeting and sensed my shock at what he'd shared. He invited me to an open conversation about my views and thoughts regarding women's roles in the church.

This isn't a story about the religious patriarchy—although I have a lot to say about it! What this is about is my decision to speak up and say something. The seed that had been planted all those years ago sprouted the night of the church meeting and in the days that followed as I examined the reality that women are still being "put in their place" in the most unlikely and sneaky spots. For years this was prevalent in my career, but now it had shown up in a place I value greatly—my church.

Remember when I said God keeps sending you the teachers until you learn the lesson?

God didn't send me to that church by accident. He sent me the mother of all Sams because He knew it would force me to get the message. And this one was my tipping point.

I'm not sure I would have had the same reaction had I not spent years climbing to the top of my career by navigating and breaking down countless established patriarchal systems and busting glass ceilings. Good journalists are trained to question and probe. As time went on, my voice got stronger the more I exercised it.

Also, I had experienced firsthand the opportunity to serve a church in a leadership role. And it wasn't just me—countless other women were doing important work ministering to people and helping churches make sound decisions.

Thinking about what had transpired with this new church, I realized I can't stay quiet. I can't keep running away when my neck gets red and my throat closes up.

I can't change a narcissist like Sam. I can't change the leadership of a television station. I can't change a church's specific doctrine. But what I can do is stand my ground and make my voice heard. I can be who I am fully—who God made me to be—and own my story and voice.

It's taken me a lot of soul-searching to really lean in and get this lesson.

The series of events that led to this awakening didn't happen by accident. Our stories are no accident.

I didn't "happen" to start a community like LIGHTbeamers and fill it with a bunch of women by accident.

I didn't move to Texas and get uprooted from everything for no good reason. Sometimes we need to be challenged to see things we otherwise would refuse to see. I was too comfortable in South Carolina. Everything I had created there was safe.

Moving back to Texas was a complete ungrounding for me. It made me reevaluate everything: my work, my circumstances, my community, my family, my relationships, my faith . . . and most importantly, my value.

What I realized is I can't run away and keep my voice to myself. I have to stand up for what I believe. I know in my heart of hearts God called me to withstand these tests so I could hone my skills to share the stories of the disenfranchised, the underserved, the overlooked, and the oppressed.

I could no longer not see what I saw, not feel what I felt.

And trust me, it's hard to speak up when, for generations, we've been told to keep quiet.

I accepted the pastor's invitation and joined him for coffee. I shared my story of being a deacon and how important it was to me to raise my kids in an environment where women are recognized and welcomed alongside men for their leadership abilities. He listened to me with grace. He didn't try to convince me that my beliefs were wrong. We simply came to the conclusion that we interpret scripture differently. He told me my views were welcome, and he encouraged me to have these conversations with more women in the church, admitting that I was not the only woman in the congregation who felt this way.

I left that meeting still a little shell-shocked yet also empowered.

In the months and years that have followed, I've come to realize the point of it all wasn't about women's equality (although it's a worthy and critical cause!) or my feminist agenda.

It was about discovering my true value, and in finding that, *I found my voice.*

Do I still attend that church? Actually, I do.

We've been attending regularly for over three years now, and trust me, I have days when I question what I'm doing there. Although the church and its people have many wonderful and redeeming qualities, I don't agree with their particular doctrine and stance on women leadership. I recently sat through the church's big announcement of its first elders being elected to office—both of them men. It's a big sticking point I've wrestled with nonstop. As someone who leads women and empowers them to share their stories and become better leaders in the world, I've felt like a fraud at times. I've had long, hard, difficult conversations with God over this one . . . and this is what I hear Him say every single time I have the urge to run away and find a new church:

"April, how do you expect to lead if you surround yourself only with people who think and believe exactly like you?"

I ran away from Sam. I left my job at the TV station. And in countless other situations, I looked for the easy way out.

We can't even begin to explore the depths of our voice if we speak it only into a vacuum chamber.

My job isn't to stay safe and comfortable anymore. My job is to call more women forward, and give them the tools and resources to discover their own value and voice. We must do this inside our organizations, our communities, our churches, and our families.

And so . . . I stay.

I stay because I trust God and I remain hopeful that I can be used appropriately as a light to others, especially for women!

Inside our LIGHTbeamers Community, we have women from all around the globe—from diverse cultures, opposing political views, vastly different backgrounds, and ways of thinking. Not once have I silenced these women from sharing their stories. I value what they have to say and give them a space to speak freely. I encourage them to test their own boundaries and comfort zones. I get them to question and probe their own beliefs and examine the boxes they may have allowed themselves to reside in a little too long.

I've created a place for them to be seen and heard. And in doing that work, I've encountered my own hard edges. My own small boxes have come into full view. I've had to find my voice in order to lead others to do the same.

It's funny to me now, thinking about women in leadership and where it has shown up for me in my life. Mostly it's been an inside job. I haven't had a lot of women leaders, especially not in my career. Most of those roles were held by men. Don't get me wrong—I've had some incredible male mentors and teachers along the way, like my two professors who heard me all those years ago when I was first testing the audible level of my voice. But I still want more. I want *more women* to stake their claim, own their story, and use their voice! There is just so much work to be done. We can't run away!

When we are comfortable, it's too easy to sit by and be "grateful" for what is ours.

When we step outside of our comfort zones, we are able to stretch and explore the depths of who we are, what we believe, and what we want to stand for. This is where we find our value and voice. No one else is going to do it for us—not even the women who are currently standing in the gap as leaders . . . because it's an inside job.

We need women leading inside our families, communities, jobs, and churches, and, most importantly, we need to lead ourselves.

The work is far from over. I'm a work in progress, too!

I don't regret any encounters or challenging conversations that have given me the opportunity to explore my voice. Some of them turned my stomach, and others made me angry and tossed me into despair. But each and every one of them gave me an opportunity to explore my deepest thoughts and my truest desires. They helped me define and claim my value and my power.

And for that, I *am* extremely grateful.

ABOUT THE AUTHOR

APRIL ADAMS PERTUIS

April Adams Pertuis has been a storyteller since she was a little girl, hiding out in her room writing secret poems and scribbling stories on the wood slats underneath her bed. An extreme sense of curiosity led her to ask a lot of questions when talking to people, wondering what secret story was hiding inside. It's no surprise that that keen interest led her to journalism school and a lengthy career as a television journalist, video producer, and brand storyteller.

In 2014, frustration over the stories being shared on social media led her on a quest to go deeper with her work. Desiring to make an impact on women's stories, she created LIGHTbeamers. Today, April leads the LIGHTbeamers Community, full of women who are curious about their own stories, and helps them excavate the layers of their stories through various online courses and coaching programs. She also hosts the Inside Story podcast, the

Storytelling Symposium, and is the co-creator of the LIGHTbeamers *She Gets Published* Author Program, all of which give women a platform from which to share their stories with the world.

When April isn't dreaming up ways to equip and empower women through storytelling, she is hanging out with her husband and two kids, traveling somewhere in the mountains, or soaking up the good Texas sunshine and eating tacos.

Learn more about April and her work on pages 325 - 331.

Chapter 2

OWN YOUR WORTH

Kristy Castilleja

"No matter your age, you are worthy of greatness in whatever form that may come for you."

All I can remember is walking into her office and being told to get on the scale. The weigh-in would determine if I was in or out. Years of diet pills, speed, diuretics, and starvation had become my way of competing in a game that was hard to win. I had been a member of my high school dance team since freshman year. Our director required weekly weigh-ins every Monday morning to see if we would make the dance for Friday night's football game. . . .

This is Texas. . . . Drill team, cheer, and football are a must in every town across the state. However, my personal game began when I was fourteen years old. Over the previous two years, I had done anything and everything to make those weekly weigh-ins. Now summer break was over, and I was walking into the dance room at my high school with dread. I had avoided all contact throughout the summer—specifically, the phone call check-ins from my line officer. I don't recall any chatter among friends as we all came back together; everyone was lined up against the wall, each of us awaiting her turn to go into the office.

I was next, and my heart stuck in my throat. I knew the result would not be in my favor.

After two years of pushing the limits of my body and my mental capacity to make Monday weigh-ins, I was mentally, physically, and emotionally exhausted. Somewhere deep inside I could not do it anymore; I could not keep up the charade. This particular summer, I had relaxed and enjoyed being me. . . . No more pills, no more deprivation. I was sixteen and just wanted to be "normal." However, the rules had changed. The weigh-in on this August morning would determine whether I remained on the team for the entire school year, even though I had made the team through a tryout process in the spring.

My bare feet touched the cold scale as she slid the rectangular knob up the bar, where it landed on 146 pounds. According to Mrs. Cody and her National Institute for Perfect Weight, I should weigh 125 pounds. This sixteen-year-old girl standing at five feet, five inches would no longer be a part of the team because she hadn't done her part over the summer . . . starved, popped pills . . . even though that's all I knew to do. I weighed 146 pounds, and I was dismissed by my director, whom I had looked up to and admired as well.

Humiliated in front of my peers, shamed and embarrassed, I ran from the room, slamming the door, forever changed. I ran and ran and ran. I got into my car and drove and drove and drove to a nearby lake. I sat on a concrete picnic table and cried, all alone. I wasn't sure how I could go on, how I could face my family, my friends, this town. I really wanted to die.

However, I didn't die. I drove back home to tell my mom what had happened. And I never went to another one of my high school football games. I lost a piece of myself that day, and I also lost a lot of respect for a teacher I had admired for two years. But I also found two incredible teachers/mentors who picked me up, dusted me off, and showed me the true value of a healthy teacher/student relationship—my journalism teacher, Mrs. Karkoska, and my golf coach, Charlie Norris. They took me into their programs after all the shaming and humiliation and loved me anyway. They emulated true educators in every sense. They were kind, forgiving, nonjudgmental, funny, and smart. They brought out talents within me that I had no idea I had—the art of writing, the game of golf, and what it means to be a good educator. These talents served me well throughout my life and are talents I still use today.

As the school year began, I asked Mrs. Karkoska if I could be in her journalism class, and to my surprise, she said yes! She actually named me the sports editor for the school newspaper and taught me the foundations of journalism: editing, headline writing, layout design, copywriting. She planted the seed of a passion in me that I'd yet to discover fully in myself. Mrs. K. encouraged me in the University Interscholastic League competition, built my confidence, and accompanied me when I qualified for State in headline writing.

Coach Norris, on the other hand, was a different personality. He had been my driver's education teacher over the summer the previous year, so I knew him fairly well. He was from Kansas and had a funny accent—at least to those of us from Texas. He was gruff, direct, and always in a hurry. I found him on the football field before school started. I timidly asked him if I might be able to join the girls' golf team that year. He asked me why I was interested. Shame and humiliation crept back in, but I told him what had happened with dance. He cocked his head, looked at me, and said, "I'll see you at the course on the first day of school. Make sure you have clubs." And off I went, immediately telling my dad he had to buy me some golf clubs.

I can honestly say that the game of golf saved me that year. It's not only a physical game, but a mental game as well. As frustrating as it was to learn not to raise my head as I hit the ball, it took even more mental discipline to trust myself. As Coach Norris patiently taught me how to grip the club, I eased into the comfort of my stance. When he demonstrated the power behind a golf swing, I practiced relentlessly, following through with my own power. All of these lessons were teaching me the game of golf, but also the game of life. My junior year, our girls' golf team qualified and played in the UIL state golf tournament for the first time in school history.

Discipline, hard work, practice, persistence, resilience, grit. Both of these teachers were instrumental in building much of who I became as a person. They truly altered the course of my life. It's taken a lifetime to see, but God had many other plans for me. He used my weaknesses to help me see my strengths.

My whole experience with dance, however, continued to haunt me. I wish I could say, unequivocally, that journalism and golf helped me forgive and forget. Unfortunately, that wound cut down to my soul. I lived too many years in shame and insecurity, desperately trying to fill in the holes left by the ravages of Mrs. Cody. The feelings of not being good enough were always in the back of my mind. Confidence eluded me. I was always searching for approval, needing other people to validate who I was, what I did, or how I did it. I questioned myself at every turn. I never felt pretty enough. I always felt fat, was always on a diet. Relationships were hard because I never felt worthy. Oh yes, the scars were deep and pervasive.

And along the way, I somehow had a very on-again, off-again relationship with God. A very strong relationship. And I know it has been by the grace of God that I am still standing today. Through many years of conversations and prayers and stillness, my daily connection with God allowed me to let it all go and to forgive. That was the hardest, after all: forgiveness.

I realized I had given Mrs. Cody all my power. I wasn't living my life to the fullest because I thought I was punishing her by hating her. The reality was that she had no idea how I felt. I was punishing only myself day after day, year after year, and holding on to something that didn't matter. It just didn't matter. I was the one who had held on to all the shame and humiliation—not her. I allowed those feelings and dark shadows to live in me, but that meant I could also boot them out.

I believe that that one moment in my life has defined much more about me than just shame. It made me strong, tough, and empathetic. It gave me skills, discipline, and perseverance. Mostly, that time gave me a frame of reference through those three teachers. In spite of the roles they played, good or bad, all three influenced me to want to be a teacher myself. I ultimately became a high school English teacher and cheer coach for seventeen years. I vowed to never make another child feel the way Mrs. Cody made me feel, but most importantly, I wanted to be the teacher and coach that Mrs. K. and Coach Norris were to me: accepting without question, kind to a fault, developing young minds as students and people, teaching not only skills but about life as well. And really, I wanted to show them love and kindness. That's really what we all want—to be validated and loved. I spent twenty-nine years in education, the last twelve as a high school administrator. Through it all, God certainly knew what He was doing. He has blessed me with a lifetime of relationships, but He also challenged me through other hardships along the way.

We spend our life chasing all that has affected us over our lifetime. What people say, how they react, and how we internalize all of it swirls around in our hearts and minds for years, unspoken, but felt day after day. What I have realized is that we have to release all that baggage and live the life that was meant for us. I have wasted much of my time giving power to someone who meant nothing instead of giving that power to myself.

My personal journey has been about building a very special relationship with God. He helped me figure my life out. It hasn't been easy, but then, why should it be? The hard stuff is what builds us into who we become; it's the darkness that becomes light; it's letting go of who we were to grab hold of who we are now. That's what God has done for me. He has built me into a woman who has emerged with experiences, triumphs, sadness, really bad lows, and some extreme highs. Building ourselves is what makes us into who we ultimately become.

When I reflect, I realize I did not have a straight path. Actually, my path has been a mess all across the universe. However, the best of times have been when I've spent time with God and really given my soul over to Him, day in and day out. My biggest triumphs have been with Him. He led me to my husband, put incredible career opportunities in front of me, and blessed me with two great kids. Most of all, He gave me life when I was at my darkest.

Although I thought, at sixteen years of age, my darkest hour had come, midlife took me to depths I had never seen before. I found myself not knowing who I had become. All of the perseverance and strength and ambition for which I had worked so very hard from my youth was now driving me out of control. I found myself overworked, stressed beyond measure with my job. My body was changing, my mind was changing, menopause was horrific, and I truly had lost my inner voice and myself in a job that was sucking me dry. Stress and worry and all the negative effects left me devoid of emotion. I found it hard to laugh, very hard to open my heart, and hard to find even a minuscule amount of joy. A pervasive sadness sat in the corner of my heart, hovering, never quite leaving, bulging out at certain times, never gone. How the hell had I gotten here? How the hell was I supposed to get out?

I realized a pattern of claiming my own unworthiness. I allowed what others said or did to permeate me. I went back to labeling myself "not enough." I married a wonderful man, but I brought my own financial debt into our marriage. As a lifelong banker, he knew debt was not acceptable. My parents had lived in debt. I remember going shopping with my mom for school clothes and her telling me not to tell my dad how much she spent. I have done the exact same thing with my own daughter—repeating a cycle from the environment in which I was raised. My husband scolded me on many occasions about my spending, but what I heard was that I am not worthy. He never said those words, of course, but that is what I internalized. I continued to spiral down into the depths of darkness of shame and humiliation. My response was to "show him" by taking the matter into my own hands and making sure I paid off my debt solely on my own. That plan, in turn, put added stress on me and silenced my voice in shame. I continued to get quieter. The pressure of paying off my debt also led me to fanatically climb the educational career ladder. *The higher I go, the more money I make, the more I can pay.*

Around the same time, in my late forties, as I was making that career climb, my boss told me that the reason I hadn't gotten a position I had applied for was that I didn't know anything. Wait . . . what? I had a master's in educational leadership. What didn't I know? Once again, that little demon on my shoulder began screaming, "You are not enough!" I overcompensated for this flaw of unworthiness by "showing him," and worked feverishly and continuously to be the best and get to the top at all costs. I climbed so far that I completely lost myself along the way. My hair was falling out, I was a zombie when I came home at night, I couldn't sleep, I gained weight, and I felt miserable. What was I really chasing? For what? For whom?

I started journaling. Somehow, I had found the energy to spend time with God again. Most mornings I began to write at 5:00 a.m., a time that became sacred because it turned the tide for me. Through meditation and prayer, I began to see my life in a different way. I slowly began to crawl out of the mire. I believe women are very good at losing themselves through their thirties and forties to their careers, to taking care of children, to running households or running businesses, or both. While trying to succeed at whatever our jam is, we lose ourselves. That was me. I had substituted success for living. I had pushed myself in my career to be the golden girl, to be the best, to show everyone that I was worthy. Yes! That was it. I had been chasing worthiness for years. Ever since Deborah Cody had said I was not worthy, I had lived a lifetime of showing her I was. I think many of us have a Mrs. Cody in some sense— someone who makes us feel or believe that we are less than who we are, someone to whom we give our power instead of using that power to believe in ourselves.

As I turned to God in my journal, little nuggets of wisdom emerged. I knew there had to be more to life than this. I prayed . . . I wrote . . . I prayed more. Little by little as I continued journaling, I kept feeling a tug on my heart. I truly wanted to do something on my own. As much as my education career had given me over the years, I had allowed it to engulf my whole being, to the point that I no longer recognized myself. Change was imminent. The thing is, when you are not in control of your life or your career, you lose power over yourself and give it to others. I was slowly realizing that I needed and wanted to take back that power. I knew God was planting a seed in my mind and nudging me along the way. I had more to do, but this time, it was for myself. I wanted to answer to no one. . . . I wanted to build something for myself. I wanted to be an example for my kids. I wanted to believe in something different from before. I could not keep spinning on the hamster wheel of crazy by doing the same thing over and over. I had to get out. . . .

Then the Covid-19 pandemic hit. Whoa! The world of education shifted—administrators and teachers were asked to do things 100 percent differently. I had to take care of 130 educators and make sure they were okay, along with 1,100 students. My perspective shifted. I became increasingly dependent on God. I knew I wanted more out of life; I needed more. I was thirsty for more. I knew I had already lived the majority of my life, so what was I going to do with the time I had left? Every day I prayed for the answers. I can't explain my relationship with God. It's very surreal and ethereal, floating out there in the universe, but the feeling is strong and powerful. I know He is guiding me, showing me the way. A calm comes over me, and I know He is there. I began to sense a direction.

As I was growing up, my parents were very social. They had lots of friends and often threw parties in our home. I loved helping my mom make food for the parties; appetizers were my thing. I crafted several recipes and learned a lot as well, particularly from my grandmother—my dad's mom. She truly was an exceptional cook, and I always wanted to learn. So began my love of cooking and entertaining. Throughout my life, I had loved entertaining, and throwing a good party with great food.

As I prayed and journaled and scoured my brain and heart for what really brought me joy, I realized it has always been making food for people and bringing them joy. As 2021 began, I thought about starting my own charcuterie business. I floated the idea with my husband and some of my closest friends. They all told me to go for it, and I launched my business in February 2021. I know this was led by nudges from up above. I felt God speaking to me: "It's your turn now—all yours."

I hit the ground running, and by April, I knew I was onto something. I kept hearing the call to retire and work my business full-time, but I wasn't really ready to retire from education. Was I? The nudges kept coming. I felt my soul ready to explode. I knew God was leading me on this path, but retirement was two years away. Faith and trust took over and pushed me into believing that I could really do it. I had read a lot about our faith in God and putting our trust in Him, but what did that really mean? It means that when you want to take a leap of faith but aren't sure, you do it anyway. It means to blindly, without any assurances, do something that is scary, unpredictable, uncomfortable.

I did it: I jumped! I went into my boss's office and told him I was retiring to work my business full-time. You know what he did? He offered me another job—one that required less time away and less stress, a job off campus with less responsibility. He dangled a carrot, so to speak, with the hope that I wouldn't turn it down. He asked me to go home and think about it overnight. What?? So I did. I went home and prayed and prayed and prayed. What I discovered is that temptation shows up in many different ways. I knew that if I truly wanted to put my faith and trust in God with this new adventure, then I had to go all in and trust that the decision I had made was the correct one. I declined the offer. I finally believed in myself enough, trusted myself enough to finally do all that I was meant to do.

Although I know all avenues of my life have been meant to be, I also know beyond a shadow of a doubt that finding ourselves again is the greatest gift of all. No matter your age, you are worthy of greatness in whatever form that may come for you. Our holes—the holes that riddle our souls—are not meant to be filled. They are meant to remain open as passages for us to travel back and forth, drawing upon our experiences. Those holes represent everything about us: who we are, where we have been, how we have handled the highs and lows and all of life's events. We continue to visit these holes so we can draw upon them and learn what to do next. They are there for us to see through, to remember, and to lead us to the other side. I am finally finding freedom in living.

Freedom is a funny thing. The minute I fully trusted God without a doubt, I was finally free. Everything I had chased all those years just dissipated. Free doesn't mean I don't suffer or struggle, but it does mean letting go, fully believing, and acting upon that belief. My hardships are my heroes; they taught me about myself and made me into who I have become. I needed hardship and struggle in my life, because through them, I found my relationship with God. And when all is still and quiet, and the birds are chirping and the clock is ticking and a silence takes hold, I hear Him speaking. He carried me from the lake that August day and has held my hand ever since. When

I choose to fully listen, I finally hear that I am enough. No more devil-speak of shame or humiliation or unworthiness; that is what the devil wants us to hear. When I am in communion with God, fully present, I am enough. Yes, I have found my voice again, passing through my holes from time to time, but still there, getting louder each day.

Although no sixteen-year-old should have to go through the experience I went through, I am glad God chose me. He knew I was strong enough to carry it, and He knew for how long; that experience was meant for me. It was meant for me to understand forgiveness, to understand giving my power away, to understand God's purpose for me, and to understand how to rise again. It has taken me years to let go and it has been a slow process, but I have discovered a resilience about myself. I have forgiven Mrs. Cody in my heart. I have celebrated Mrs. Karkoska and the kindness she showed to me, and I have thanked Coach Norris for teaching me the game of golf and so much more. Those three will never know the true impact they have had on me over my lifetime. God has shown me how to be me and only me. And that is enough.

ABOUT THE AUTHOR
KRISTY CASTILLEJA

Kristy Castilleja grew up in a small East Texas town where school was always a refuge of friends, learning, and a favorite teacher or two. She loved to dance, hang out with friends, and ride the country roads. High school became a different story when a single act by one of those favorite teachers changed her life forever. Resiliency, strength, and faith led Kristy on a path to find herself again. Throughout her journey, she struggled to find her own worthiness, until her faith in God led her to true peace. Her story is about how educators—good and bad—influenced her and led her to a lifelong career in education, despite hardships. Kristy taught high school English and coached cheerleading for seventeen years before becoming a high school assistant principal, academic dean, and middle school principal. She retired as a high school principal.

As Kristy begins her second act in life, she has taken a complete leap of faith and started her own business. She wants other women to find their voice in becoming who they were meant to be without fear or shame or doubt. She believes that knowing your self-worth is the first step in starting life anew, regardless of age. To find out more, visit Kristy at www.kristycastilleja.com

Chapter 3

ALLOW YOURSELF TO BE SEEN

Leanne Smith

"Self-respect was waiting for me to look in the mirror and find it."

Mirror, mirror on the wall. I don't look at you at all.

My bedroom was dimly lighted, causing shadows and dark corners, just the way I liked it. My mirror was hidden by an open closet door, making it easy to avoid my reflection. In the darkness, I pulled open a dresser drawer and saw a pair of bright hero-printed leggings with a waistband that boldly proclaimed "Girl Power." As I picked them up with sweaty palms and a pounding heart, I thought, *What was I thinking?*

But I knew what I was thinking, because I overthought and obsessed about everything. My mind was a constant spin of thoughts that made it hard for me to focus. I was constantly thinking, but my mind was a blur of misfired random thoughts that led me to worry.

I had some things to worry about. My marriage had spiraled into a difficult separation, our family farm was in peril, and my financial career was in jeopardy. I worried about my children. How could my son and daughter learn self-confidence and self-respect when I didn't have it myself? My life felt like a house of cards teetering on the brink of collapse.

In my comfort zone, I could control everything; as a result, my comfort zone became smaller. My life became rigid and tense. *The more I played small in my comfort zone, the less chance the real Leanne would be seen and open to attack.* I memorized. I perfected. I shrank my goals and dreams. I made excuses for failed attempts and then readjusted to lower my standards. I became comfortable settling and retreating in silence to pretend everything was perfect. Except it wasn't.

I was exhausted, and caring about myself was too much effort.

I did not get enough sleep. I drank an obsessive amount of coffee. I stopped working out. I gained weight. I developed an anxiety rash. I bought big, baggy, dark clothes that allowed me to hide. I stopped looking at myself in the mirror.

The mirror was something on the wall that I glanced at. I would check to see if my shirt was wrinkled, if I had spilled something or had crazy hair sticking up, but I would *really* not look at myself. I would do my makeup quickly in the morning, in a memorized way that allowed me to be efficient and required little evaluation. I would not make eye contact with myself in the mirror. My reflection held the truth I was unable to face: I did not respect myself enough to make myself a priority.

I had many rationalizations for why I did not need to worry about myself. I would have time for me someday. After all, I had two children who were busy. Their activities filled up our calendar. My daughter's days were filled with dance. If she wasn't at a dance lesson, she was practicing, or making up her own choreography. Hip-hop songs continually filled our house, and the furniture was often moved to allow for a dance party. I was busy working all day. My evenings were for housework, laundry, driving to dance lessons, watching her dance moves, and loving her enjoyment of dance. Who had time for anything else?

One late fall night we were driving to dance and talked about the possibility of her doing a hip-hop solo that competition season.

"That is scary," she said.

"It's just new, not scary," I replied with fake confidence. "Do you love dancing?"

"Yes."

"Do you love hip-hop and dance it all day every day?" I asked.

"Well, yeah," came the reply.

"Does your instructor think you can do a solo?"

"Yes. But Mom, what if I fall?"

Instant panic in the pit of my stomach from the image that flashed in my mind. Everything in me wanted to say, "You won't fall." The superwoman version of me wanted to swoop in with a promise of perfection that would make it all better.

Instead, I swallowed hard to settle my quivering voice and asked, "What does your dance instructor say to do if you fall?"

"Get up and keep going."

At that moment I was sure my daughter's dance instructor was an angel sent to save a wannabe superwoman. With a sigh of relief, I said a silent thank-you for all the times the instructor had instilled in her that if she fell, she needed to get back up.

"Then I think you should do what you love and what you are good at. You just need to decide to do it," I said with renewed confidence.

"Okay," she said as she hopped out of the truck.

As my daughter skipped into the dance hall, I was filled with anxiety. All the words rang true, but I felt like a fake. I had just been given the best advice when I was supposed to be the one giving it. I sat in my truck alone in the dark winter night. The darkness was my solitude, allowing me to hide from myself and ignore my truth. Truth and honesty are my values, and I was wanting my children to be courageous, active, and happy . . . even though I was not. I was terrified of failing and avoided it at all costs. I was living vicariously through my daughter.

I looked out my truck window and saw the reflection of the brightly lighted dance hall. My daughter was in there dancing in a room full of mirrors, watching herself move, getting continual feedback on her performance, hearing what she was doing wrong, and working to improve. She was inside living. I was on the outside looking in.

How could I encourage her to be brave and bold when I was used to the safety of the dark, being content without happiness, and avoiding my reflection?

My overthinking brain did not let go of the realization that I was unable to mirror the truth I wanted my daughter to learn: perfectionism isn't real, and pursuing it gets in the way of happiness.

Sitting there in the quiet night, I decided to find a way back to living my own life with choices to find fun and happiness again. It sounded bold and brave . . . and instantly set my mind into anxious thoughts: *But how?*

These thoughts were on a continuous loop in my mind, so when I saw a bright poster for Zumba in a shop window that proclaimed it was possible to "party yourself into shape," I was interested. Music, a fun party, and getting into shape sounded like all of my favorite things. While still standing in front of the store, I dialed the number on the poster.

It rang once. Twice. *Oh my gosh, what have I done?* Three, my nervousness rising. *Why did I spontaneously call?* Four. Perfect—*no one is answering.* Five. My heart was beating so loudly, I could barely hear myself leave a message.

Hanging up, I was happy with my brave moment of spontaneous action. *No one returns phone calls,* I assured myself as I continued with my farmers market tour. As I was walking back to my vehicle with fresh vegetables and flowers, my phone rang. Distracted and juggling my shopping bags, I dug into my purse and pulled it out, absentmindedly answering even though it wasn't a number I recognized.

A cheery voice greeted me with "Hello, I am returning your call about wanting to take Zumba classes."

Oh no, I thought, stopping in place. *Who is this person who actually returns phone calls?* But I was quickly caught up in the whirl of her high-energy enthusiasm as I listened to her describe her upcoming classes.

In a moment of wild abandon, while I was on the phone, I signed up for a Zumba class that was happening the next day.

All night and through the next day, I overthought the situation. My mind became a tangled mess of thoughts that all ended in reasons to stay home. Why was I joining this class by myself? Did I have anything to wear? What if I couldn't do it? What if I was off course and crashed into someone?

When I arrived at the class, the music was pumping with a language I didn't understand, and I was definitely thinking the decision was pure insanity.

The beautiful instructor, Gaby, greeted me enthusiastically. "Leanne! I am so glad you could join us. Come up front so you can see me."

The front row? *Oh, I don't think so*! my mind screamed silently. "I'm fine back here," I stammered.

"You will see better and be able to watch me. Come."

As Gaby was guiding me, I noticed that the front of the room had full-length mirrors down the entire wall. I stumbled in fear. Normally I didn't even look into a mirror, and here I was face-to-face with a wall of them. *What was I thinking, signing up for this?* ran through my mind for the thousandth time. I could feel the lump in my chest growing. My palms were sweating, and the music was quiet from the pounding of my heart in my ears. My plan of sneaking in, and then staying by the door for a quick getaway in case of a wardrobe malfunction, was fading.

Being at the front had one benefit, I thought. I wouldn't have to make eye contact with anyone in my stumbling . . . I mean, dancing.

Zumba, Gaby informed me, had a repeating choreography to an eight count. The dance mom in me breathed a silent sigh of relief. I had watched countless hours of my daughter's dance practice, silently counting and memorizing her routines. My brain was tired and wired, but all I had to do was count to eight. I could do this.

The party disco lights started, reflecting off the mirrors in a pattern as rapid as my heartbeat. The tempo of the music increased along with my anxiety.

The first song was an oldie (in English!), and I knew every word. My feet had no clue what to do, but my mind relaxed with the familiarity of the lyrics. I moved. Awkwardly, but I was moving. The song changed, and in the dark, except for the flashing disco lights, I relaxed a bit. I was sweating, and not from a panic attack. I lip-synced. I giggled as more lyrics brought back old memories.

Then it happened: I felt my leggings slip.

My mind flashed to a nightmarish dance competition wardrobe memory of one of my daughter's jazz costumes. That year our costumes arrived later than normal, and when we received hers, it was so big, it fell off of her. Under examination, I discovered that the outfit had a 44 bust size. My daughter was eight years old. Needless to say, she didn't fill out the costume. I quickly shipped it off for fast alterations to get it back in time for the first competition of the season. I picked up the newly repaired costume, and we drove to our early morning competition.

We arrived in the changing room for our dance school, and while my daughter went to get changed, I was thrilled to see a few of my dance mom friends. We started to visit while the girls changed, and I was lost in catching up with them.

Suddenly I heard a high-pitched "Mom! My costume DOESN'T FIT!"

I felt the blood drain from my face as I turned around to see my daughter, eyes full of tears, clutching the costume to hold it up. The costume was still way too big. One jazzy move and it would be in a pile on the floor.

"No problem," I said matter-of-factly as my eyes looked over my daughter's head and locked onto my friend's eyes. "We can fix this right here."

My daughter was looking extremely skeptical when my friends leapt into action.

"No problem."

"We'll have this fixed in just a few minutes, honey."

My dance mom friends are a special group—spunky, confident, and sprinkling laughter and smiles with their vibe. And trust me, their vibe is bold and joyful. Our exuberance and jumping into immediate action silenced my daughter's doubts. There is also a strong possibility she knew there was no stopping us once we were on a mission.

As we circled around my daughter, words started to fly. Would safety pins work? Who had a needle? Did anyone have thread this color?

All of a sudden my friend grabbed a tube of instant super-hold fabric glue from the depths of her dance bag.

"How fast do you think instant hold is?" I asked.

"We're about to find out," she said.

We worked in tandem, grabbing material, folding it, and using what seemed like a crazy amount of fabric glue. All the while my friends talked about the competition, how lucky my daughter was to have such long, beautiful eyelashes, how the soup at the concession sounded great, and the running update on our dance club's standings. Nonstop chatter to entertain and distract from the fact that we might be gluing the costume to her skin.

"Perfect and maybe even better than the original," my friend declared as we backed away to inspect our alterations and send my daughter off to the last rehearsal before competition time.

"Do you think it's glued to her?" I mumbled in a sigh that was both relief and worry as we watched her run off to join her friends.

"If it is, we'll figure out how to get it off of her," came the reply.

If I had any doubts in my mind, they weren't about my group of friends or my confidence when I was with them.

I'm so unprepared, I thought now as I frantically grabbed at my own slipping waistband. *Why didn't I pack fabric glue? Where are my dance moms to rally around me in a wardrobe crisis? Who knew I would need a wardrobe support team for Zumba?*

I awkwardly shimmied and tentatively shook while pulling up my slipping pants. I looked over at Gaby. How was she able to cha-cha-cha with no pant malfunction?

After class Gaby came over to speak with me. "Lovey, how was the class?"

I found myself saying that I loved the class but needed to find better clothes so I could move more freely. "Your pants didn't slip at all, and mine felt like they were falling off."

"Oh yes! Pants made by Zumba are the best—they just stay put and don't slip down. They let me not worry at all about my moves. I can just shake it, shake it."

Really? My new friend was sharing the secret to not worrying about dance moves and it involved shopping for new leggings? Sign me up.

While I still had massive workout endorphins rushing through me, I found out how to get my own pair of Zumba pants and excitedly signed up for the next class.

But the excitement I felt after the rush of the workout wore off. By the time I was standing in my dimly lighted bedroom a few days later, I felt less excited and more scared. I reached into my dresser drawer and picked up my bright new leggings, which were as beautiful in color as they were in message. Girl power had seemed easy when I was on a post-workout high, but now, in the darkness of my bedroom, self-doubts crept in. My closet was full of shades of black, and my new leggings were so bright, I thought they might glow in the dark. I wanted to stay in the comfort of my bedroom and hide. Going out in public with an outfit that drew attention seemed bold, and made me so uncomfortable, I wanted to cry.

Why did I think new leggings would be better than a bottle of instant-hold fabric glue for my old ones? How was I to be confident without the sparkle and smiles of my friends? How were bright new leggings going to make it okay to step into that room of mirrors, dance patterns, and high-vibe energy?

"It's just new, not scary" flashed into my mind. Why did my exhausted mind that had problems remembering what I did yesterday remember that conversation with my daughter? Especially at this moment when I wanted to give in to my fears and stay home. I clutched my bright pants as tightly as I clutched my fears. I knew if I wanted to be an example for my children, I had to take responsibility for my action and inaction. I took a deep breath and, with tears in my eyes, got dressed. I had stayed in the dark long enough.

I wiggled into my new leggings and adjusted them without looking. I glanced down and felt a wave of insecurity. Undoubtedly this was the most attention-getting outfit I owned. I intentionally left my closet door open, which hid my mirror so I could avoid my reflection as I walked out of my bedroom.

I drove to Zumba, and as I stepped out of the vehicle, my eyes landed on my pants. I was used to monitoring my words and movement so I wouldn't draw attention to myself, and this outfit was like a neon sign proclaiming my girl power.

I slipped into the class and edged toward the back of the room.

What if people thought I was pretending to be something I wasn't? Who did I think I was, dressing like a Zumba instructor? Was I acting like I knew it all and was perfect? I felt like a fake.

Walking into the dance studio for another dance workout, I heard a voice. *"Hermosa!"* ("Beautiful!") "You are a superhero! You look beautiful in your new outfit. Trust me, you will love your pants."

I still had my head down, lost in my thoughts, when I realized that my new friend and Zumba instructor was calling to me. I felt my cheeks blush. I was so far out of my comfort zone, I could not even accept the compliment. But I did trust Gaby with her bold exuberance.

The class started, and I tentatively shook in the first salsa song. Nothing happened. A small sigh of relief. I gained some confidence and moved more. Nothing slipped. In fact, I felt better than I had imagined I could. I recognized the first songs from the previous class and started to enjoy myself.

The music switched, and the song had new choreography that had us crisscross our feet and end in a dip. Counting to eight was suddenly impossible. I was off count, stumbling, and my arms were flailing. Panic set in. I was so far from perfect and being in control, I could feel my embarrassment rise. My mind spun, and I was convinced I should not have come to the class. I avoided all eye contact and decided this was the longest flamenco song in existence.

The song ended, and Gaby laughed. *"Hermosuras"* ("Lovelies"), she said, laughing, "I don't have this new song perfected, but it is so fun. We will work at it and be better next week."

There was a collective sigh of relief and chatter of agreement among all of us dancers: yes, it was fun, and there was definitely room for us to improve next week.

A new song started, but I was still thinking about her words in amazement. My admiration for Gaby was growing. She did not have the song perfected, but she had put it in the playlist anyway. She didn't let perfection stop her from having fun while she was improving. Why did I expect myself to be perfect when I was just learning?

It was as though a permission slip to just have fun and be happy had been handed to me.

My brain chatter slowed. My shoulders relaxed. My arms started to follow my legs. Halfway through the class, I looked at the mirrors in the front of the room. My gaze was drawn to fun, bright colors and a smiling dancer.

I smiled automatically at the happy image.

Wait a minute, I thought, blinking as the smiling person in the mirror blinked back. *Is that happy person actually me?* I was learning to let go, and it showed on my face, the way I moved, and the ease in my smile.

I was looking at myself in the mirror.

For the first time in a long time, I was really seeing my reflection and watching myself move toward happiness.

Staring at my new girl power Zumba pants, I knew they were a statement, a vibe that spoke to my style: happy, bright, and positive. But it was more than that.

My smile was wide, authentic, and a layer of vulnerability was cracking wide open. I was waving my hands higher in the air. The music sounded louder because my heart was not pounding in my ears. My feet felt lighter. The pulsating strobe lights fed my energy level. My tired and wired mind started to ease into the simple task of moving to a beat. I clapped at the end of the song as much for the other dancers and the instructor as I did for myself. I felt my circle of friends growing and shining bright in the disco lights.

Dancing in the Zumba class, I found my happiness with girl power leggings, party lights, and a salsa shimmy. I discovered that self-respect was waiting for me to look in the mirror and find it.

I became comfortable in my bright, colorful pants and wore them all the time to Zumba. One night a few of us were walking to our outdoor class when one of the ladies' daughters, who was about nine years old, came up to me.

"I love your pants!" she said.

"Thank you so much."

"My mom should get a pair of pants like that, but she isn't into fun," the girl said as she walked beside me.

Her words landed deep. I understood not being into fun. Fun can be scary and make you uncomfortable. When you are busy balancing a house of cards, you don't have time for fun. Fun feels light and bright, and when your world is dark and heavy, it can be overwhelming. I had been busy trying to be superwoman when I just needed to be into fun.

"Hmm, well, my teenage daughter thinks these pants are a bit too fun and bright," I replied.

The little girl looked at me in as much disbelief as amazement and shook her head as she walked away.

That adorable girl didn't understand black pants as I did. Black pants had been my comfort zone costume. Zumba had pushed me beyond the edges of that comfort zone. It helped me release my fears of being too much, too awkward, too bold, and too fake. It reflected my smile back to me. Now I easily wear leggings as loud as the music to remind myself that I have learned to be happy being me, with gratitude, grit, and girl power.

I continued making my way to the park where the class was happening. As I was greeting everyone, another Zumba friend said, "I need to hurry and stake my spot to dance."

"Oh, me too!" I exclaimed, and I made my way to the front row beside her.

As I was picking my spot to shake and shimmy, I realized that I was in the front row of my life and not hiding in the back row anymore. I had moved from monocolor to technicolor. My circle of friends with a bold and joyful vibe had expanded. I was participating in my own life.

One day, my daughter brought two of her friends home for lunch, and soon food, backpacks, and girl chatter filled my table. These girls were part of my daughter's circle who sparkle and shine together, so I left them to their conversation while I worked. I was at my desk with my back to the teenagers, typing and partially listening as they talked about clothes, food, homework. Suddenly one girl made a comment about her face and not liking how she looked that day. My mind spiraled with the familiarity of the words and took me back to my own struggle with the mirror.

The trip back to my self-doubt was swift. Had I really made improvement in myself if, in a few words, I could easily remember what it was like to dislike and avoid my reflection? I closed my eyes in a flash of panic. The words had been said matter-of-factly, with a sense of belief and acceptance. I had fought the battle of low self-esteem too hard to just sit quietly and allow those negative words to settle in my home.

I needed to say something to instill in these girls the knowledge that the power of self-respect lay within them. While I was searching for words of encouragement— something that wouldn't sound like a boring mom lecture—my daughter interjected.

"Don't say stuff like that around my mom," she said. "She'll say something lame like 'Don't disrespect your face.'"

Hearing her use my words told me that my battle for self-esteem did matter. It was important to remember my old self so that I could appreciate where I was now, which was far from where I had started. Realizing that others see the light I am reflecting made the battle worth winning.

Smiling wide, I turned around and said, "Yeah, respect your face. If you don't, no one will."

Mirror, mirror on the wall, I respect you after all.

ABOUT THE AUTHOR
LEANNE SMITH

Growing up, Leanne could happily spend hours getting lost in a story with her Walkman, listening to an eighties girl-power mixtape. Wearing her go-to outfit of neon leggings, high-tops, and leg warmers, Leanne thought she would never stop believing that girls just wanted to have fun. Then, as a mother of two teenagers, Leanne realized she was avoiding her reflection in a mirror and dressing in black. She'd lost her happy spark, and having fun was on her back burner.

Leanne believes that when you live your story full out, you choose to be a force of happiness. Today, as a Jack Canfield Success Principles trainer, she coaches women in how to step into their power by reclaiming their self-worth. If Leanne is not adventuring off-grid, she is wearing bright pants and doing a happy dance. Connect with Leanne at www.absoluteleanne.com

Chapter 4

RISE ABOVE CONDITIONING

Pamela Meadows

"To move in the direction of your dreams and who you want to be five years from now, let go of the expectations that others have placed on your life."

The air was crisp on that fall day—the kind of day that makes you think of apple cider and pumpkin pie. With the dogs resting at my feet and the kids milling about in the living room, I looked out my home office window. Exhausted, but perfectly content, I placed the last checkmark on my long list of to-do items.

As I began to prepare my list for the next day, I glanced at the calendar. *PTA board meeting tomorrow? Already?* I scrunched my shoulders. No point in complaining. I had to go.

My home office was neat and organized, unlike the living room on the other side of the office door, which was scattered with blankets and shoes. Backpacks dropped carelessly blocked the entrance to the kitchen. *One more thing to clean.*

Time to check my mental to-do list: cook dinner, sign school papers, and listen to the kids tell me how their day at school had gone. I loved our tradition of sharing our highs and lows, and I was always grateful for dinner together and thankful for dishes to clean because it meant we had food to eat. Still, the list of housework was never-ending—one more dish to clean and one more load of laundry to start. It was all so tiring.

Dinner over, the last dish washed, and a load of laundry chugging away to a steady beat, I made my way to the bathroom, glad to wash the day away. I turned the shower knob to the hottest setting and undressed, exhausted to the bone.

Stepping into the shower, I pondered my constant fatigue. It was all my fault, the result of never saying no to anything. I was in the place I'd dreamed about: flourishing in my corporate career, taking on each challenge, accepting every assignment. I couldn't pass up an opportunity to grow professionally, and, admittedly, I never wanted to disappoint anyone at work.

Work brought exhilaration along with challenges. It was all the extracurricular activities that drained my energy. The PTA board, Pop Warner football board, this board, that board. Boards needed volunteers, and everyone knew I was a guaranteed yes. I wanted to be known as that mom—involved, committed, and engaged in the lives of my children.

It didn't stop at work and school. On Sundays, I led the three-year-olds' Sunday school classes. Those cute little faces lured me into yet another commitment on my only day of rest . . . my Sabbath. Every yes I offered to others was a no to myself, my needs, my self-care.

I was a people-pleasing perfectionist who thrived on external validation. No wonder I felt exhausted.

I challenged my waning energy with the same old lie: "Isn't that what a good woman is supposed to be?" I bought into the superhero motif of a woman extended far beyond herself—selfless, worn out, and overwhelmed, clutching her weariness like a badge of honor, proof that she had done enough, given it all. I wanted to be the epitome of female excellence. So why did I feel wrung out like a dishrag?

The to-do lists had become a distraction from the inner voice whispering to me to stop, recharge, and renew my spirit.

What was wrong with me?

A good woman. That was the paradigm that had guided my actions up to now. The type of woman who sacrifices herself for her husband, children, career, and community. That is what a good woman does—abandoning the essence of herself for the greater good of others. I wore the mantle, the heavy cloak. I smiled when people conferred the titles upon me: "good girl," "good wife," "good mom."

When I looked down at my skin, I saw that it was scalded red. I had felt no pain when the steamy water hit me, but now, seconds later, the sting was growing.

The irony hit me like a jolt of caffeine. I wanted the shower to be the place where I melted off the weight of the day; instead, it had burned me.

As I jumped back to escape further injury, I felt the hot tears crawling from my chest to my neck and pausing just behind my eyes. *What a metaphor for my life.* Everything meant to bring me comfort was burning me out.

I was living the life women are taught to crave. I was checking off all the boxes. Crushing it at work: check. Respected member of my community: check. Doting wife and mother: check. I was functioning from a numbed reality for the good of my family, work, and community. I was not just exhausted and frustrated; I was resentful as well.

The tears broke free, soaking my soft cheeks and dropping onto my chest. I knew with every fiber of my being that I had to make a change. I turned the shower knobs to warm, stepped back under the water, and felt immediate relief.

I had remained numb so long, every emotion was identical. Pain was equal to joy. Disappointment was the same as success. Exhaustion was just like breathing.

That is the answer, my heart screamed. I would not live one more day beneath my joy, reaching up from the pit to steal a gasp of air before being buried again beneath the obligations I had piled on myself.

The unrealistic standard of what a woman *should be* dissipated like the mist in the shower that day. I wanted a life that brought me joy. I wanted to say yes to my true purpose and no to other people's priorities. I would break out of the cage that had become my life.

Significant work would be required to dismantle the cage I had willingly erected. I chased recognition and praise to feel love, and paid the price for embracing all the "rules" of what it meant to be female. I pursued security and inclusion and lost individuality and purpose.

The only thing standing between where I was and where I wanted to be was the story I told myself about what women "should be."

Conditioning

Reflecting on the teachings I received and the beliefs I held from my youth, I realized that I had been conditioned to meet the societal standard of a "good girl." Well-meaning family and unquestioned societal standards shaped the essential characterization of "good" in my mind. I never questioned my elders. They defined the standard, and I worked to meet it:

- Be polite.
  Is something or someone making you uncomfortable? Just smile, look away, and don't make a big deal out of it.
- Be proper.
  Ladies always cross their legs, they do not cuss, they do not wear anything too revealing, and remember, "You catch more flies with honey than vinegar."
- Be selfless.
  Be everything to everyone. Being a good girl means caring more about other people's needs and feelings than your own.
- Be modest and grateful.
  Good girls don't brag. It's unbecoming to take credit. Remember always to have a happy, humble heart and be grateful for what you have.

Please don't misunderstand; those traits are good, but they should not come at the expense of your self-respect, intuition, or ambition. As "good girls" grow up, we carry these beliefs with us out of childhood into adulthood, where they morph into the philosophies by which we live.

The problem is, they don't always fit adult life.

Be polite
Politeness may come at the expense of being direct and protecting yourself.

Early in my career, I worked with a male colleague I'll call Bob who became too flirty. One day, I was working from home when he messaged that he missed seeing my pearly-white smile in the office. I responded with a smiley-face emoji and let him know I was working from home because my kid was sick and my husband wasn't able to take the day off. I thought that by mentioning my husband, he would get the hint. Not Bob! He persisted, messaging that I should wear jeans to the office when I returned because I made the office look better on casual Fridays.

I ignored some of his messages, hoping my silence would speak for me. Other messages I responded to by mentioning my husband again. I was trying to be polite. But he was undaunted by my silence or references to marriage. One day, at a corporate event, Bob came over and placed his hand on my lower back, just above my bottom. I froze. The polite, good girl training told me not to make a scene. I smiled and eased away from his grasp.

I finally worked up enough courage to go to someone in the human resources department.

"What have you done to let him know this is not acceptable?" she asked.

I considered the gravity of the question, ashamed of myself that I had not yelled at Bob or looked him directly in the eye and said, "Stop! You are making me uncomfortable." My need to appear polite prolonged my distress. The person in HR told me I would need to bring the issue to our CEO. Fear gripped my heart. I was scared to talk to the CEO, because Bob ranked much higher than me in our organization. The polite gene was in hyperdrive. I didn't want to appear disrespectful.

But I worked up the courage, and fortunately, the CEO listened. He reviewed all the chat messages and spoke with Bob.

Regret rose inside me. I had let myself down in failing to take a stand. Bob's harassment had worked because I valued politeness over dignity. I had worried about being seen as emotional, reactive, and inconsiderate of Bob. I had subjected myself to months of feeling uncomfortable because I did not want people to think I was impertinent. Although Bob was the aggressor, I had looked for ways to respond softly or covertly so as not to upset him.

When the reality of that sank in, I felt nauseated. My concern over protecting my harasser had led me to judge myself as overthinking, hysterical, or creating a problem for him.

I was fascinated by this phenomenon and wondered how many other women sacrificed the protection of self for the protection of an abuser. My research revealed that I was far from alone. In 2018, the Rape, Abuse and Incest National Network found that 69 percent of sexual assaults are not reported. In the remaining 31 percent of cases, less than 6 percent of the offenders are ever arrested, and of those arrested, less than 1 percent receive jail time.

This was not just my problem; this was a systemic, cultural, societal crisis. Girls who are taught to be polite, to not upset people or make a scene, may inadvertently hear that their feelings, intuition, and safety are less important than someone else's embarrassment.

Women who want to establish their place in society must have a well-developed sense of self-respect and a hefty amount of confidence. Politeness cannot be the enemy of poise, courage, and self-esteem.

Be proper
Being proper may come at the expense of being introspective, curious, and inclusive.

Glancing at my colleagues seated at the corporate boardroom table, I silently judged the woman—let's call her Michelle—sitting across from me when she leaned over and whispered to our male colleague. *How unprofessional*, I thought. At one point, she blurted out that someone needed to "get their shit together." That was the only expletive she would utter in the hour we spent in the conference room.

Michelle even had the audacity to meet friends for wine after work, letting her kids get off the bus and inside their house by themselves, and leaving her husband to take care of dinner.

I was astonished and mentioned it to my husband, who confirmed that he would certainly not want to be married to a woman who spoke and behaved that way.

Although I felt a pull to know better, I lived in a black-and-white world around those who helped to shape my opinion and confirm my belief system.

Women who are taught how they should behave become easily affronted by women who break the mold by being loud, assertive, and vivacious.

They just want attention! I would think about the woman at work who would go to the cigar bar or golf with men from the office. *What are they trying to prove?*

These offenders of the good girl code sometimes wear tight-fitting pants suits or short skirts. The good girl training protests, *They're just looking for attention*! The "be proper" paradigm turns out to be little more than a big setup for women; it creates competition and judgment among us. It happens so subtly, so instinctively, we don't even realize it.

Really, who cares if that woman golfs with the guys? Good for her for having the drive to compete! Who cares if that friend drops the f-bomb? Good for her for expressing her thoughts freely! What do another woman's clothing choices have to do with me? Absolutely nothing. What do I know about their character from those few decisions? Absolutely nothing. So why would I compete with or judge them?

Be selfless

Selflessness disguises our inability to establish boundaries and comes at the expense of our goals and dreams. Our weakness and lack of self-preservation enslave us to bad ideas and obligate us to commitments we would reject if we ever found our voices.

Selflessness was defined in the invisible good girl handbook as being more concerned about the needs and wishes of others than your own. But that citation needed a footnote that warned women not to care so deeply about other people's opinions and desires that their needs were subjugated to them.

There was a time when I said yes to everything that I believed I should do or that a good wife, mom, or employee should want to do.

"Pamela, we would love it if you would join the PTA board!" came the cheerful request from a fellow inmate in the prison of the good girl idea.

I would rather stick shards of glass in my eye is what came to my mind. What came out of my mouth: "Of course—count me in!" I flashed my smile (willing it to be heartfelt) to match hers and was committed to another obligation I didn't want.

Then came the sports boards.

"Glad to help!" I tried to convince myself that was true.

"Pamela, we need this report finished tonight. Can you support that?" came the request for another late night of work.

"Absolutely—count me in," I would say, even though I knew it meant getting the family settled and then another all-nighter.

I disappeared into all the roles, buried by an avalanche of shoulds. I moved from one to the next without ever checking in with myself to ask, *Hey, self, is this what you want to do? Does this bring you any joy?* Glennon Doyle sums it up best: "Women who are best at this disappearing act earn the highest praise: She is so selfless."

As I voluntarily faded into the scripts written for me, I feared that I had lost myself. I was not sure if I knew who I was anymore. Then I learned that we are never lost to ourselves. We simply need to tune in to the deepest parts of our being and remember who we were before we believed who "they" said we should be.

I read somewhere that "ships don't sink because of the water around them; ships sink because of the water that gets in them." If we think about belief systems as the water and ourselves as the ship, we realize that we begin to sink when we let those external belief systems into our sacred vessel.

Be modest/grateful

Modesty often comes at the expense of advocating for yourself.

I have excelled in my career, and thought, in the early years, that my ambition to achieve was healthy. After all, doesn't everyone want to be successful? So, I stuffed my days with hustle, constantly overdelivering.

Enter promotions and pay raises, which led me to believe this constant hustle produced positive results. The busyness was served with a side of ceaseless feelings of being a complete fraud, an imposter bound to be found out. The solution? Hustle harder. The hustle, the never-enough-ness, and the imposter syndrome are three heads of the same monster.

Women need to move away from the addiction to motion and the need to please others and learn to be aware of what our real priorities are.

While I worked tirelessly, I lived in fraud mode and accepted consolation prizes in the form of advancements instead of advocating for myself.

Women are taught to be modest about their accomplishments and gratefully accept whatever they are given. Although gratitude is incredibly important for a happy life, it is possible to be grateful while simultaneously wanting more. It is not *either/or*, it is *and*.
To excel at work, earn promotions, and gain pay raises, demonstrate and share your accomplishments. Go ahead and be grateful for where you are, but be visibly prepared to step into the next opportunity. According to a study published by *Harvard Business Review* in 2014, women do not apply for jobs because they believe they are not 100 percent qualified for the position. Women choose to, instead, be modest and grateful for where they are in their careers. Stop waiting—promote yourself. Shine, and shine brightly.

I was determined to stop living in the prison I had built for myself—caged by bars, each representing a "should" in my life. I would make a conscious effort to build a life by design, not by default.

This was not an easy task. I had to move from my unconscious, reactive beliefs to honestly explore where my philosophies and thoughts originated.

I needed to understand what I assumed about topics, what I believed, how I felt, and how I wanted to behave in response. I asked myself what fundamental truths I wanted to serve as the foundation of my belief system. The answer was clear: acceptance.

It was always acceptance that I desired most deeply. That is why I was afraid to disappoint others in my life. I conformed rather than accepting myself as I was.

Cleansed of the conditioning, I could evaluate each thought or belief to see if it was tied to a "should." If it was, I challenged it.

Our thoughts are shaped by our environments, such as family, friends, education, community, and society. I learned that thoughts are just thoughts, and they can be changed. Changing our thoughts updates our beliefs, transforms our feelings, and subsequently influences our behavior.

A simple flowchart helped me plot backward from the "should" behavior to the feelings around the behaviors/beliefs, and ultimately my thoughts on the subject.

Thoughts ➡ Beliefs ➡ Feelings ➡ Behavior

This flowchart was the starting point of the methodology I developed to track my thoughts before they became beliefs and actions. It was powerful and effective. So I felt it deserved a name. I called it the DIG System.

DIG In

In my career as a vice president of quality and compliance, I love to analyze the root cause of an issue, build flowcharts, and trend data. Leveraging my love of quality, I built DIG on the premise that challenging our beliefs, thoughts, and assumptions opens our minds to explore and get closer to our truth. Then we can align our behavior with what is real to us instead of aligning with unchallenged assumptions.

With this flowchart in mind, and the understanding that beliefs are just the thoughts you think most often, let's explore DIG.

> **1. D = Discover.** Ask yourself, *What beliefs are leading me to this thought, reaction, or feeling?*
>
> Early in my career, I struggled with comparing myself with other women.
>
> I began dating my husband at age twenty, and we married a couple of years later. Because he is eleven years older than me, I valued his beliefs and experience. In those early years, his guidance helped shape my beliefs about how women should behave, including what we should or should not do. Recalling his words, I denounced the golfer/cigar-smoking colleague

for not being home with her family. Surely, I thought, she had her priorities confused.

DIG required me to question if *I* felt the same way and ask myself which of *my* beliefs were leading me to compare myself with her and regard her with contempt. What I discovered led to a reframing of the situation.

You can be a woman who likes golfing without trying to be "one of the guys." Arranging for your partner to take the evening parenting shift so you can network and bond with your coworkers does not make you a bad wife or mom. I can celebrate her choices—or even make the same ones—instead of succumbing to the comparison/competition trap. Although going to a cigar bar is not my idea of a good time, I would absolutely drive the golf cart!

I made an intentional decision to create my own thoughts and beliefs around this situation and change my behavior from self-righteous and judging to open and accepting.

2. I = Investigate. Ask yourself, *Why do I feel this way?*

To really explore why I felt competitive or frustrated with other women, I had to ask that same question more than once to dig deep enough to find the answer. One thing I discovered was that it all came down to conditioning, environment, and other people's lenses.

I decided to listen to my gut and pay attention to my own experiences, using them to shape my beliefs.

I asked myself how I felt about women—their wardrobes, hobbies, hustle, and priorities, and I came to one general conclusion: I support them, period. I am here to celebrate and encourage women to be diverse, to be courageous, to be honest thought leaders. All women have a right to be heard and respected, not just the "good girls." The irony is that the "good girls" are often the women who have been conditioned to stay small and quiet.

Think about the stories we would miss if all women complied with the "good girl" rule.

The girls and women who dare to listen to their aspirations, thoughts, and beliefs despite being told what they "should" do are changing our world. They have sacrificed broad acceptance of others to achieve acceptance of themselves.

What thoughts and aspirations do you have that, if you allowed yourself to believe in them, would move the needle for yourself and for the women who are inspired by your courage?

3. G = Ground. Ask yourself, *Does this reaction correlate to who I want to become?*

My old reactions of judgment, internal comparison, and jealousy were not aligned with who I wanted to be. I wanted to be successful and have a happy family while also building a strong friend network, able to say no when it felt right and say yes to the things that lighted my soul on fire. I wanted to be able to make room for myself in my life without feeling guilty.

To ground yourself, ask who you want to be in one year, three years, five years. Ask what it would take to get there, and then start thinking, acting, and living as if you were already that future version of yourself.

The future version of me is a fierce and fearless advocate for women, and in that version, there is no room for competition or for jealousy of my sisters who are out in the world living their truths.

People live their lives as a result of the stories they believe about themselves—the stories they repeat in their heads and hearts. I believe we are doing the best we can with what we know and that as we learn more, we can grow and change. As we evolve, the people around us are presented with the opportunity to embark on their own paradigm shifts. My husband has matured and changed many of his youthful views on how a woman should behave and, for that matter, how a man should behave. He and I still have many opposing views, but we work to listen to each other. It is not always easy, but we are committed to understanding each other.

I am no relationship expert. My marriage has seen its share of ups and downs. At times since our wedding in 2005, I have thought, *I can't do this anymore.* Still, here we are, taking small steps toward each other, deliberately and, at times, nervously addressing each other's thoughts and behaviors.

I believe if we keep making space for honest, hard conversations and are committed to listening with acceptance as the goal, then we can continue to grow together.

If we can DIG and grow, then we have a chance to upend our conditioning.

As I worked to reduce people-pleasing tendencies, I learned the power of the word *no*—two little letters powerful enough to be a complete sentence. *No* can transform you from exhaustion to alignment. *No* can help you shed the shell of your past conditioning to be what others determined for you. *No* can help you define who you are rather than being defined.

I also have created a word hack. Instead of saying "I should," I say "I choose to." I no longer do what aligns with *should*; I do what is life giving, electrifying, and energizing—the things that I choose to do. No, I don't evade my responsibilities or the hard things in life. I just reframe how I think of them. For example, I should change the toilet paper roll so no one gets stranded. But I change it because I *choose* to and also because of karma.

Not every task passes the "choose to" reframing. I stepped back from the PTA and chose to not join the board again. I still choose to be a card-toting member of the PTA, willing to bake and provide donations when it is convenient. But I have shed the pressure that I *should* do more. I do enough. If all women (and men) were willing to do enough for the PTA, I think there would be a lot fewer stressed board members.

In the workplace, I am still up for a challenge. I want to grow professionally and be a team player. I know now that I can do all these things while insisting on appropriate boundaries. I would never have said no to an assignment before, and in general, I take on challenging work assignments. The difference is that I now say something like, "That sounds like a great challenge! I'm working on [fill in the blank]. Which of those should be de-prioritized so I can work on this new assignment?" This allows coworkers to know what I am working on but that I'm willing to help while setting realistic boundaries and expectations. Another benefit of this exercise is that it keeps me aligned with the most crucial work tasks.

I use the DIG method every day. When a negative, judgmental, or defeatist belief pops into my head, I discover the thought behind it, investigate where it is coming from, and ground myself by asking if this thought, belief, or potential action would help me become the woman I want to be.

I am grateful for the journey that I have been on. I no longer hold judgmental beliefs against myself and other women. I deeply understand the importance of breaking free from those limiting beliefs. I can be more open-minded and accepting of myself, of women, and of men. We are all doing life together, and although we are not always on the same path, we can be empathetic with one another.

What stories about yourself do you need to DIG into?

Key Takeaways

Today I feel it all—the full range of emotions. It is the blessing and burden of no longer being numb. I can feel the sting of disappointment, but I can also feel the dizzying elation of success. My yeses come from my soul now and are backed by the alignment with my personal mission. My shower burns from that fateful day scabbed over. Beneath the scabs, nature was doing its magic trick of creating new skin. Similarly, I was working beneath the surface to enliven my spirit. I dug deep to unearth the treasure buried below. That's the way it is with treasures— they are often buried. But a buried treasure can never be spent. Only when it is excavated, brought to the surface, and opened can it truly be enjoyed.

Social conditioning was the soil that hid my treasures, causing me to forget who I was. Now that I am free, and getting freer each day, I work to help free other women from the "shoulds" that have covered their gems—the best gifts they possess that they could be using each day to change the world.

To move in the direction of your dreams and meet the person you want to be five years from now, let go of the expectations others have placed on your life. The world does not need carbon copies trying to out-hustle one another or win each other's approval; it needs people committed to continual growth, coloring outside the lines, and free from limitations—people who are living at the height of their purpose and passion.

ABOUT THE AUTHOR

PAMELA MEADOWS

Pamela's life was fraught with the belief that she had to be perfect, she had to please people, and she had to work hard for approval. Between the unfulfilling hustle[, battling imposter syndrome, and saying yes to everyone but herself, she was burned out and felt lost.

Fortunately, Pamela stopped looking to everyone else for direction and turned inward. She learned that she was enough and had agency over her life, and understood she could be herself without apology.

The transformation that Pamela experienced encouraged her to dig even deeper. While still an executive at a large organization, she became a certified coach. Pamela knows too many other women are stuck on the hamster wheel of feeling obligated to "do it all," worried about other people's opinions, and listening to that nasty inner critic.

To learn more about Pamela, follow her on Instagram @pamelameadowsoptimist

Chapter 5

WALK OUT OF THE DARKNESS

Julia Barton

"My healing was in the form of self-transformation, shedding the old and making room for the new."

Flowers would most likely be one of the answers you would receive if you were to ask my friends and family what first comes to mind when they think of me. And rightfully so, because I adore flowers and find their process of growth intriguing. Flowers evoke colorful feelings within me, feelings of pure joy. Yet I can sadly say that there once was a time when flowers did not bring me any pleasure. When I should have been relating to a blossoming flower, I felt much like a seed—a seed buried in the depth of darkness, burdened by the heavy soil above. My heart felt numb; it lacked happiness. The lack of emotion within scared me, to the point that I worried I would forever be lost in the darkness, unable to navigate the dirty, daunting path toward the light. I nearly convinced myself that no one would notice or even care if a flower was missing from their garden.

In a month or so, my husband and I would be expanding our garden to make room for a beautiful baby girl. The past few years had been filled with both excitement and exhaustion. We were building our dream home. My husband was working hard seven days a week. I was home alone with an active three-year-old son, and dealing with daily sickness from the pregnancy. I miraculously sold our old home on my own without a real estate agent. It was painful, but we had to let go of our builder, who also happened to be a family friend. We were homeless for just over a month. We were both grateful to be working through the process together, but it left us weary. I knew I had to stay strong for my husband, my son, and myself. I knew I had to take what I'd been dealt, as tricky as it was, and not let it get to me. Super-emotional woman that I am, I somehow made it through without breaking down. I was proud of myself. It had been like a test, and I had passed.

I had dreamed of moving into a fully finished home, one where we could enjoy ourselves as a family of three and relax in the weeks before the baby came. Well, the reality was very different. We ended up moving into an unfinished home. Cooking and preparing food without countertops is an art, so we soon opted for plywood to get by. I scrambled to unpack boxes before the baby arrived, a task made difficult with no shelving or hanging rods in any closets. I was disgusted at the idea of having to live out of boxes. I was sick and exhausted, and all the disorder left me feeling defeated. But I had to suck it up, although I felt I had done more than my fair share of that lately. I had to not let it bother me and just look forward to having this baby and feeling good again. We tried our best to bury our roots as deep as possible to build a strong foundation for the new addition who was about to arrive.

In the morning of September 1, 2016, I started having contractions. My husband came home from work and took me to the hospital. I thought it would be quick, as did the nurses and doctor, since it was my second birth. I was very wrong, and endured hours and hours of arduous labor. I so badly wanted to give up. I did not have the willpower to continue but felt I was disappointing the doctor and nurses. I was doing all they asked of me but making little progress. I did not have the strength to keep going, but I would not let myself fail. I feared that if I were to show weakness or admit weakness to myself or others, I might not be able to give birth on my own and the doctor would need to use forceps—maybe even do a cesarean, which terrified me. I took some deep breaths and set my mind to birthing this baby naturally.

I did it. I gave birth to my baby girl a day later. She was a big girl and born faceup, which can make for a particularly hard birth. After learning why her labor had been so burdensome, I was able to feel pride, knowing I hadn't given up. A strong wave of relief swept over me. I was looking forward to better days, days of not feeling sick. I could not wait to go home and start feeling good again. Our garden was now complete: we were finally a family of four.

People would think we had it all, that we were rooted and blooming with joy, with a new dream home, a sweet baby girl, and each other. But instead, we felt depleted; my husband was exhausted from constantly working, and I was still feeling the weight of it all.

I had always needed to have all my plants in equal, straight rows, looking neat, clean, and orderly. Well, my current garden was far from being the organized space I had once been able to keep. Lots had gone as planned, but lots had not. The things that had not gone as planned had gotten the best of me, making my mind spin out of control. I couldn't pretend or hold it in anymore.

Contractors were in and out of our house during the workweek, invading my personal space. I had to breastfeed my daughter in my bedroom so I could have privacy. I would get frustrated when my son left the door open. I would panic at the thought of it being too noisy for nap time. My son needed a nap, and most of all, *I* needed a nap. Rest time was crucial for us all. I especially needed a nap to help me get through the rest of each day. Without it, I felt I would crumble to the floor. I would feel anxiety and rage if something stood in the way of our nap.

My nieces, who were about eight and ten, would sometimes come over unexpectedly on the weekends, often around lunch and nap time. I loved the thought of them playing with my son and having family close by, but the timing was off. I did not do well with unexpected things, especially with people over near or during rest time. I found myself panicking, asking my husband to please ask them to leave because my son and I needed rest—now.

Rest time was the *only* thing I could control, and I did everything in my power to make sure it happened. Sleeping was my safe, quiet space; it was the only time I could be without chaos, the only thing I seemed to succeed at, despite my many failures.

I felt much like a seed, buried in the depth of darkness, burdened by the heavy soil above.

My house, life, and kids were far from being orderly, organized, or calm. Instead, I was feeling angry, overwhelmed, and out of control. I regularly snapped at my three-year-old. I struggled to focus and found myself unable to handle almost everything, even small things. I sobbed uncontrollably every day. I thought I was a horrible mom. I wanted to be an angel; I didn't want to keep living here on earth. I thought no one would care whether I was here. I wanted to die. I felt so alone. I struggled with myself, not knowing why I felt this way when I should have been feeling happiness and joy. I should have been taking satisfaction in all the beauty that surrounded us. I was finally in our new home, and our family was complete and perfect, but my surroundings were not bringing me the joy I thought they would.

My husband gave me loving support, day in and day out, no matter how crazy I was or how crazy things got. I called him multiple times every day, sobbing and telling him, "I just can't do this anymore." He would come home early when I couldn't bear another second alone with the chaos that consumed me. He helped me when I needed to breastfeed at night and was exhausted and did not want to. He would listen to all my sorrow and hold a safe, loving space for me. He worked at finishing up projects around the house when I thought that having projects finished would help. He would take my son to work on the days I could only, just barely, handle taking care of myself and the baby. He would comfort, care, and be completely there for me. He exceeded at giving me the support I needed from him.

But something was still missing. I yearned for a mother's love. I wanted my mother's shoulder to cry on. I wanted the luxury of being able to call her when I needed to talk or receive advice. I needed her to tell me that it would all be okay, to say I was doing a great job. I wasn't, but hearing encouraging words would have been enough.

I was close to my mom growing up and never thought I would be going into motherhood without her maternal support. I knew my mom couldn't be there for me as she and I both wanted, but it hurt so deeply that the pain was unbearable. Our situation was complicated, and we were not communicating for reasons I can't go into right now. I was not able to just call her when I needed to talk. I grieved not having her by my side, even though she was alive. I had to accept that she was not in a place to give me support, leaving me to navigate the darkness and this new journey alone, not knowing how to be a wonderful mother like she had been to me and like I had once been to my son. I hoped for brighter days ahead, the ability to poke out of the darkness toward the light.

As I sat at my computer one day, I saw something about postpartum depression, or PPD. I read it and wept uncontrollably. I finally realized why I felt like a complete mess. I looked up PPD right then and there, reading as much as I could, educating myself. I then started calling around to find a postpartum therapist.

Unfortunately, I was not successful at finding a therapist who specialized in PPD support. However, I was able to get in with my primary care physician and figured she would help me find someone. I talked with her about what was going on, and took a test. But I left out some details, like not wanting to be here anymore, because I feared I might be hospitalized and ultimately separated from my family. She gave me some names of general therapists in the area and a prescription for medications. It wasn't the direction I wanted to go in, but I graciously took both the list and the prescription. I needed to get rid of the hurt, pain, and sorrow; I could not go on this way.

After learning more about what might be going on with me, I found myself germinating toward hope. I briefly shared what I was experiencing with my dad and stepmom and then with my husband's parents, hoping for guidance or much-needed support. I started seeing a therapist and taking the medication, feeling hopeful but also doubting it would help. I wanted nothing more than to receive help and support, but I chose not to tell my close friends what I was going through. I did not want to spoil the time I spent with them. Although I was numb to everything but pain and grief, I put on my best happy face to enjoy my time with them as a way to escape from it all. I did not talk about any of the craziness happening with me, because I didn't want to admit weakness or seem ungrateful.

I was scared to death that I would never bloom into the wonderful mother I wanted to be for my daughter. I wanted to experience the joy and beauty of this precious time. I wanted the same happiness I'd felt after my son was born; I wanted the old me back.

I was seeing a therapist one to two times a week, but it was not helping. I could have just talked to a wall and made more progress. Instead, I wanted and needed support with purpose. The medication was taking the edge off, but I just did not feel like that was what I needed. I knew deep down I was dealing with much more than just PPD. For years I had not allowed myself to experience healthy emotions while building our home and feeling sick during my pregnancy. I did not release or process it, for fear of showing weakness or being ungrateful. I had buried it all so deeply, trying not to feel the pain, that it had made me numb. I was past the point of processing, and I was in no frame of mind to do anything of the sort.

Less than six months after starting the medication, I decided to stop taking it, hoping to find a way to get myself through and heal instead of covering up the pain.

For reasons pertaining to our daughter, I decided to book an appointment with a psychic medium. I was pleasantly surprised to receive encouraging messages from spirit guides and loved ones who had passed. During my reading, I felt loved, supported, and heard by those who surrounded me in spirit. I walked away feeling refreshed and hopeful. I thought to myself, *This might be the help I need.*

After the reading, I grew stronger each day, although I still grieved the lack of support during my darkest moments. I kept asking myself why our families did not help after we told them what I was going through. For example, I wondered why my mother-in-law wouldn't stop in after I told her it was too much for me to take the baby out to visit her. I'd see her drive by multiple times a week to help my sister-in-law and brother-in-law, who lived next door, with their children. This is one of my most painful memories, and it's still hard not to shed a tear when I think about it. I remember sitting on the edge of my bed, nursing my daughter, while seeing her drive by and hoping she would stop to visit with us.

I could not comprehend asking for help; I was merely struggling to get through each day, yearning for support but not even thinking to ask for it, much less knowing how to do so. Did I not receive help because I didn't ask? Was it because I was a stay-at-home mom? Because my husband and I seemed to get through most everything without help? Was it because people didn't know how to support or help me? Or because they thought it was basic baby blues? I danced around all the possible reasons but did not have the answers and was not in a position to ask family members the questions. I knew it was not anyone's fault, but I was hurt. I think things could have worked out differently if I'd felt surrounded by the love and support of my family during this difficult time. Trying to rationalize it while still profoundly feeling it led me down the path of not feeling worthy of help. I ultimately told myself I wasn't worthy of receiving support, whereas others around me were.

During this time of reflection, I vowed to myself that when I felt good again, I would help other new moms after the birth of their babies. I would help others without them having to ask for help, knowing what new moms need and caring for them. Giving to others brings me great joy, so I knew that someday, having learned from my experience, I would help others. I would help others with postpartum support. I said, "When I feel good again, I want to become a postpartum doula," because I didn't want anyone to feel the way I did. I also envisioned myself making house calls in a vintage car. Crazy, right? I saw myself giving the support new mothers so desperately needed, because I knew what it was like to feel unsupported and lost.

I grew stronger and more resilient as each year passed—making room for new growth and new beauty, and taking in the light. I was on a path of healing. My healing was in the form of self-transformation, shedding the old and making room for the new, being okay with not ever being the same as I was before my daughter was born. I wanted better: to feel better and to be better. Being a goal-driven person, not wanting to disappoint others or myself, I set out to make things Bloomin' Happen. I saw my psychic medium often, working through the pain and grief. I received messages from spirit guides and loved ones who had passed that gave me strength and let me know I was supported, even from the other side. My readings were a form of therapy, and I left each session feeling encouraged.

But it was not all sunshine and daisies, and sometimes all I could do was weep. My tears flowed downward as though watering my roots, knowing they needed water to grow.

I worked on releasing the pain of not having my mother in my life to be there and help me on this challenging path of motherhood. I finally started to process all that had happened leading up to the birth of my daughter. I worked on closing the wounds of not receiving support from our families. My psychic medium and I also chatted about my dreams of supporting others during postpartum, in hopes that they would soon manifest. I was digging out all the stale matter inside me, making room for fresh new contents. I found the process of talking and looking back very painful, like growing pains. But I pushed on, because I knew it was what I needed to feel good again.

I was budding toward doing things for myself, things with purpose. I saw an advertisement for a wellness craft fair at the wellness center my psychic owned, and even though I didn't know how I would make it happen, I signed up to have a table. I had no clue what I was thinking; I just knew I needed to do something that made me happy—and crafting made me happy. Why not make some items for the fair? So that is what I did. I spent several weeks creating coasters, wall art, essential oil products, handmade cards, essential oil boxes, and much more. I set my mind to it, and I made it happen. I had a beautiful spread of all kinds of handmade pieces to offer at the wellness fair. It felt great and brought me joy, because I could focus on something other than mom duties.

Shortly after crafting items for the fair, I read in our local newsletter that our farmers market was looking for a new board member. I called and set up a time to discuss the opportunity. I ultimately accepted the role and served my community while getting much-needed time away from the house. I was looking for ways to have a purpose in life other than being a mother.

I ended up having the best time at the craft fair and worked hard at creating a new business. I found myself making new products and booking craft fairs and other events. I enjoyed supporting my local community and loved my time away, meeting new people in the new town we now call home.

During this time, I also created a couple of events: Purposefully Crafting Your Bloomin' Future and Purposefully Crafting Your Bloomin' Self, intended to help women and moms. The events involved making a craft and guided conversation about taking care of yourself, making time for yourself, and manifesting goals. I still was not entirely through healing, but I felt like I needed to get things rolling. Part of my healing was to have purpose and feel worthy of taking time to do other work, even if it was volunteering for free or not exactly bringing in the big bucks. It gave me something to look forward to, and it gave me hope that there was more.

As I was working on these new things, I noticed that I was starting to be surrounded by more and more people who gave me support, love, and joy. I was beginning to feel again; it felt new and raw. I started feeling happiness, after having had to fake it for so long. It had taken years to get to this point, and I was proud of myself. I knew I had more work to do, but I was still proud that I was seeing and feeling progress within. I felt like a bud, getting ready for the transformation of blossoming.

And just like that, it seemed like I found myself blooming among a bountiful garden of supportive, beautiful friends. Even though it was the dead of winter here in New England, I felt warmth, and saw the light and beauty around me. It had been four and a half years since I had given birth to my daughter—years spent growing into a better mother, business owner, and community volunteer. I felt accomplished after pushing myself beyond my comfort level. I was enjoying motherhood. I loved my new business and the joy it brought me. In the process of growing and ultimately blossoming into the new and improved me, I was able to attract like-minded, loving, and supportive friends who stood by me, friends who cheered me on, supported my new business, and helped when they saw I was in need—friends I can proudly call family. I cannot fully put the feeling into words, because it was something I had not ever felt. Finally, I was able to be me, and knowing that people liked me, flaws and all, was utterly delightful.

As I thought back to my darkest days, I realized that seeds need a period of dark loneliness to grow. They need the weight of the soil above to help them stay grounded. They require darkness to find the light. They need to be alone to grow independently into their own beautiful, unique flower without being compared with others.

It was still winter when I happened to see a postpartum doula course starting in just a couple of weeks. My husband and I discussed it, and agreed I should sign up. Our schedules were pretty jam-packed, but if there is a will, there will be a way. I was scared at first, not knowing how I would manage everything. Had I not learned over the past few years that I should not take on too much? However, those thoughts did not stop me. I felt unstoppable and exceedingly determined. I wanted to make things happen.

During the nine-week doula training, I signed up for multiple classes on topics ranging from essential oils for new moms to Reiki certification. I had taken Reiki 1 when I was around eight years old. However, I wanted to continue my practice by taking the Reiki 2 certification and Reiki master certification. After searching, I found that the teacher with whom I had taken Reiki 1 was still offering classes, so I happily signed up for both. I was amazed that somehow, I completed my courses with lots of help and support from my husband, friends, and some family members. I was so proud that I was not feeling overwhelmed by doing it all. The inner joy it brought me, all the healing and self-work, had helped it fall into place without being stressful. For the first time in a long time, I felt worthy of amazing things.

I knew in my heart that I needed to plant more seeds to share more. I completed all my training and then needed to think of a business name. It needed to represent who I was and what my mission was. Then one day, after lots of other considerations, it came to me: Olive & Bloom. Olive is one of my favorite colors and symbolizes peace and harmony. According to Anne Christine Tooley, on energyandvibration. com, olive green speaks of "space and wisdom, feminine leadership qualities, and peace through compassion for humanity." Bloom represents my love of flowers and my journey. I fell in love with the name. It had so much meaning and encompassed me and the journey that had brought me to this point.

I was still dreaming of that antique car—a vehicle to make house calls with, a moving billboard that could bring awareness to postpartum support. I searched everywhere, and stumbled upon a listing for the most fabulous 1953 Chevy Bel Air in the most beautiful shade of blue. It was beyond our budget, so I had no hope of getting it and moved on to look at others. But to my surprise, my husband thought we should look into it. It was not a project car, which he liked a lot. He liked the fact that we could just get in it and drive. After everything worked out in our favor, we hopped into the truck, trailer in tow, and brought it home to New Hampshire from Pennsylvania. To no one's surprise, I named her Olive. Olive is more than just a car; she is a symbol of hope. She makes me feel alive, alive with a promise to myself for another tomorrow. She shows me how to keep moving forward, no matter what difficulty stands in my path. Olive makes me smile.

I was giddy with the thought of making my dreams come true, and it felt unreal. Although it was a new feeling, I was starting to feel worthy of receiving beautiful things. Wow: I never thought any of this would happen or that I would get to this point. I had completed my training, picked a business name, and bought the car of my dreams—all while still dealing with the daily ins and outs of raising young children, being a stay-at-home mom, being a business owner, and serving my community, among many other things. I was proud of myself. I had accomplished so much within several months. I was proud of my focus, drive, and purpose, because I would soon use it all to help others.

A plentiful, beautiful garden is meant to be shared. I now have the new titles of postpartum doula and Reiki master; Olive, the car of my dreams; and the perfect business name. I am overjoyed that I can share my story, my business, and myself with others. I honestly never thought I had even a chance of being graced with making my dreams come true.

Much like a flower, I needed water, light, nutrients, and a supportive environment to help me grow and bloom. Although growth never ends, I was *finally* the blossoming flower I'd always wanted to be. I finally feel that I have a purpose. My purpose grew during one of the most difficult periods of my life. I learned so much about myself through my transformation from seed to bloom. For instance, help and support sometimes come from unexpected places. I realized that I do better with loving support surrounding me, because I can finally admit to myself and others that I cannot do it all independently. I am able to ask for help when I need it. Although I may still struggle with it, I can now say, "I am worthy."

My postpartum training taught me, among many other beautiful things, that in addition to a new baby being born, a new mother is born. My Reiki master training taught me how to heal others while also healing myself. The mediumship sessions taught me that I am supported by spirit guides and loved ones, even though they are not physically here with me. When I look at Olive, I am reminded of the will to make things happen and not give up. When I say my new business name, I am so proud of what I've started, and I can't wait to see where it leads me. I am so humbled by the help and support I've received in making it all happen.

I wrote this story on the fifth anniversary of the birth of my beautiful daughter, the day I, too, was birthed into a new mom and woman. Although I wanted to give up and at times did not want to be here on earth, I was graciously given the will to survive. I survived and bloomed so I could help others sow their seeds so that they, too, can grow and bloom into motherhood while receiving love and support.

ABOUT THE AUTHOR

JULIA BARTON

The seeds of Julia Barton's life mission were planted when she earned her Reiki 1 certification at the age of eight. A born intuitive and empath, young Julia used Reiki to make herself feel safe and protected. Despite growing up in a holistic household, she found in her adulthood that she was unsure how to best use her gifts. That all changed when she started a family. Her isolating experience with postpartum depression cultivated a desire to support and nurture others. She became a postpartum doula and Reiki master to offer love, warmth, and support to help new moms trust their intuition and find joy throughout their postpartum journey. Julia's desire to help women bloom into their fullest selves became a business: Olive & Bloom Holistic Care and Healing.

Find support for yourself or someone you love at www.oliveandbloom.net

Chapter 6

LIVE AND GRIEVE WITH COURAGE

Deb Cummins Stellato

"Grief never becomes a well-healed scar. But it doesn't have to be an open wound."

Sometimes you choose your story. Sometimes it chooses you. This is the unwanted, unexpected story of my 364-day grief journey. A story told in snapshots. The indelible pictures of an unimaginable year.

I have always loved the power of a photo. I'm an amateur at best. My photos allow me to reflect on the meaning of time and place. I am the person in my family always begging to take the group photo. I struggle to delete any photo on my phone.

My love of pictures began with a tradition: the family slide show.

It was always an ordeal to get the slide show set up. My father would have to drag out the awkward green screen that probably weighed fifty pounds from the basement. We'd have to find the right table to place the carousel on. My parents took the time to ensure that the images were perfectly positioned for us to view.

After finding a seat on a black folding chair, we excitedly awaited each snapshot.

Slide shows were our family's version of sitting around a campfire. They would often include cousins and extended family. There was great storytelling. It was how I learned about the history of my family. My mother's summers in the mountains and crystal-clear lakes of Canada. My father's winters in Miami.

Memories of a place captured in a split second. Snapshots of time that circle through my head like that slide carousel of my childhood.

Snapshot. I'm a Jersey girl.

I grew up in northern New Jersey. A place where in the sixties and seventies, men jumped on regional trains to go to work in New York City. I grew up in a place that loved Bruce Springsteen. I grew up in a place that had once been farmland. I grew up in a town called Woodcliff Lake . . . which was actually a man-made reservoir.

The beaches of northern New Jersey became the portrait of my teens.

Jersey girls spend summers at the "shore" . . . not the beach. As a teenager, I loved nothing better than throwing my baby oil into a bag and taking a day trip with friends.

Snapshot. My college graduation and my twenty-first birthday. My parents announce that they are separating. Impeccable timing.

I was not surprised. As a child, I never thought of my parents as a happily married couple. Fiercely competitive with each other, theirs was a relationship of one-upmanship. The tension between them had always been palpable. My brother and I had learned to just live with it.

I was oddly relieved that they had finally given each other permission to go their separate ways.

The plan: My mom would stay in our house in New Jersey. My dad would be taking a new job in scenic Saratoga Springs, New York.

After graduation, I became a permanent Pennsylvanian. Leaving my Jersey roots behind, I would juggle the two-hour ride to visit my mom and the less regular four-hour drive to see my dad.

Snapshot. Saratoga Lake at sunset. For over thirty years, we visited my dad and his new wife in Saratoga Springs.

Their house sat high on a hill with a clear view of a sparkling lake. I was mesmerized by the calmness of that water. The stillness of the place.

My adult relationship with my dad consisted mostly of weekly Sunday calls and check-ins.

The visits to Saratoga were filled with predictable annual activities. Visiting the thoroughbreds that ran the track. Indulgent ice cream excursions. Pausing to appreciate the sunset together. Traditions that redefined my relationship with my father later in his life. In some ways, time realigned my expectations of him. I found it easier to be his daughter as an adult than I had as a child.

Snapshots clearly define each decade of my life. Snapshots become your memories   . The carousel is the place where these memories are stored. This catalog becomes your story.

I taught my daughter, Alli, about the power of a snapshot.

"Close your eyes and take a mental picture of this moment to remember it forever," I would tell her.

Taking your snapshot requires you to be fully present and in the moment. It is a powerful way to grow gratitude.

I can close my eyes and see the snapshots of places that have brought me joy. And, of course, the overexposed photos of pain.

These snapshots evoke powerful emotions. A mental time machine. A highly curated photo album of places that have defined my most sacred memories.

Snapshot. September 19, 2018. My snapshot became an indelible, unforgettable, heartbreaking, and unimaginable picture.

The night before, my husband, Mom, and I had shared an intimate and lively traditional Rosh Hashanah holiday meal. She had made matzo ball soup. We shared a loaf of challah that we dipped in honey for a sweet year.

In a family of intellectuals, I loved the banter that happened on nights like these. That night, we were immersed in a conversation about the Supreme Court. The selection of the next justice. The state of our judicial system.

At eighty-three, my mom was the smartest person in every room she walked into, and she would tell you so. A lively evening in our home was filled with intellectual curiosity and debate. That was true that evening in mid-September.

Mom always wore her stunning marquise-shaped engagement ring on her right hand after her divorce from my dad. Without it, her beautiful hands look naked. That night, she was not wearing the ring, not wanting to mess it up in the matzo meal mix. I noticed it, but didn't think much of it at the time.

I wasn't feeling well, and we made it an early evening. Sinuses. I knew I wasn't "on." If I had had my way that night, I would have stayed home and gone to bed before the sun had even gone down.

But that would have meant disappointing her. Again.

Being together for the holidays meant everything to my mom. When she divorced and moved to Pennsylvania to be closer to Alli and me, we worked hard to create new traditions.

We are not practicing Jews. But cultural traditions have always been important in my family of origin. Some years we were invited to a local Reform synagogue to partake in the services. We had skipped it this year, choosing instead a table full of food, love, and family.

Our plan was to spend two consecutive nights together. My mom had chosen to entertain us on the first night, and we looked forward to her visit on the second evening of the Jewish new year.

My husband and I headed home that evening. I complained about my headache. And felt guilty about the lack of sparkle I had brought to the evening's celebration. And, I did what I almost always did after spending time with my mother. Especially when I didn't give a full "performance "When I wasn't totally "on." I called her when we got home to thank her for the matzo balls and challah and our time together. She didn't pick up the phone. That made sense. It was around 9:00 p.m., and she loved taking a nice, hot shower before getting under her lush sheets and blankets.

So, I sent her a text. Which she didn't respond to. Again, I didn't think too much about it, because I thought she was probably asleep. She didn't have the kind of 24/7 relationship with her phone that we did.

When I woke up the next day, my text hadn't been answered. There was no message. I began to worry.

I was keeping it together, knowing that I would see her at our house later that day for our second celebration.

This had happened before, this lack of response. And it had always scared the crap out of me.

My mom was the model of perfect health, rarely going to a doctor or taking medications. She walked her two tightly wound Tibetan terriers up and down her driveway (the length of a ski slope) at least twice a day. She jogged in place while brushing her teeth or cleaning the dishes. But she lived alone.

On those occasions when she hadn't responded, I'd jumped into my car and driven the twenty-five minutes to her house. In those twenty-five minutes, I created a plethora of stories in my head.

She had forgotten to charge the phone.

She had left the phone in the car.

She had left the phone at home.

The loudest and most constant story was that she was mad at me. That I had somehow disappointed her. That it was somehow about me.

I was a dutiful, attentive, and loving daughter who adored her mother. But I never felt like I got it exactly right with her. It was hard to explain, but it always left me in a place of apologizing. I constantly questioned myself. How could it be that all that I did out of choice never felt like enough?

As I flew down the highway that morning, my heart was racing.

Because the other story that played in the soundtrack of my mind was that something had happened. Something bad.

She lived in a 5,000-square-foot house at the top of a mountain, alone. She refused to lock her doors. If I ever mentioned the purchase of a little item called a medical alert system, she would go ballistic. We had begged her to consider downsizing, but our concerns always precipitated a fight.

So, we had stopped arguing with her. "The only way you will get me out of this house is on a stretcher," she would say.

So here I was, once again . . . a crazy woman driving like a bat out of hell to her house, talking to myself out loud and wondering why she wasn't responding. As I got closer to the house, I got angrier and angrier. And more and more afraid. My heart was pounding out of my chest. As I pulled up the driveway, I noticed that the two terriers were not on guard in the window.

I had a certain knowing in that moment that something might be terribly wrong.

I entered the house and began calling her name. I ran throughout the first floor. Looking in every bedroom, her office, the kitchen. When I entered her bedroom, I found both dogs in her closet, shaking.

I ran upstairs, feeling like my body was going to collapse underneath me. Then I ran back downstairs, where I pushed open the gate to the basement stairway. A trail of dinner napkins were scattered on the steps. And when I got to the bottom of the stairs, I saw blood splattered on the white wall.

Snapshot. There, at the bottom of the steps, facedown, with her head turned to the side and one eye barely open, was my everything. My mom. She was still alive. But not responsive. Every part of my body knew that I had lost her.

I don't consider myself to be good in a crisis, but I jumped quickly into action and immediately started making phone calls. 911. My husband. Then 911 again . . . screaming at the EMS attendant. *Where are they? Why is it taking so long? Yes, the house is hidden in the woods. Get here now. She is dying.*

Throughout it all, I held her hand. When the person on the other end of the phone got quiet, I wept, begging mom not to leave me. I looked into her eyes. I knew she knew that I was there. She had waited for me.

Less than twenty-four hours passed between finding her at the bottom of the stairs and saying goodbye to her in the trauma unit. I held her hand as she crossed over while my brother stood at her feet.

My mom died on September 20, 2018, of a traumatic brain injury from a catastrophic fall down her basement steps. That perfect brain would be what killed her.

The image of her on that floor in that moment with that look in her eye became the worst kind of snapshot. One that would haunt me in the middle of the night. One that would wake me from a dead sleep, crying hysterically with a kind of pain I had never in my life imagined.

I was totally unprepared for any of this. I had never even considered the notion that my mother was mortal. That she would die. And that I would be left with a hole in my heart.

When we're facing other milestone life moments, we prepare.

Some couples go to counseling before walking down the aisle. We go to parenting classes. We read how-to books on everything except dealing with death.

Nobody prepares you for the sudden and single most tragic thing that will ever happen to you.

The details of my mom's death consumed my life for six months. I prepared her house to go on the market. I waded through mounds of paperwork and memorabilia I had never seen. I coordinated a team of professionals to clear out what remained of her belongings. During those six months, I felt like a project manager. I would spend each day in her house simply sorting through a life that had been rich and full.

When March came, I knew I needed to separate myself from the day-to-day tasks of taking care of all the "things." I knew that if I didn't listen to my body, my head, and my heart, I might not pull myself together. And I needed to pull myself together, because my dad was dying. We were making tough decisions about his health care and hospice.

I was in the middle of a grief journey. And a crisis of the soul.

That is when the next pivot of this year of grief began.

I knew that if I couldn't find my inner compass, redefine my sense of self, and become whole, my pain would consume me.

I became focused on a mission to heal my soul.

Because more important than being someone's daughter is the importance of being someone's mother.

Snapshot. My daughter, Alli, has been the constant North Star in my life since her birth on September 20, 1990. Every decision, every pivot, every vision I've had in my life has been about showing up as the best mom I can be.

I divorced Alli's dad when she was a tot. The label that she always carries with her is one that she did not choose: child of divorce.

My daughter, my mother, and I functioned as a constellation. Three stars burning brightly, gaining source power from one another.

The most important piece of the healing process was being fully present with the love of my life, my daughter.

What I didn't know was that reclaiming my life would come from a sacred place in the woods.

Yes, I had journaled. I had a wonderful grief therapist. The people in my support system wrapped themselves around me like a warm blanket. My husband wiped my tears every night when I would relive the evening of September 19 in my nightmares.

But there was something I needed that only I could choose. It was a space to heal.

My mother had taught Alli and me two specific modes of self-care: shopping and pampering.

Alli and I chose the latter.

And so began our relationship with The Lodge at Woodloch. A gem nestled in the tall trees of Pennsylvania.

Snapshot. A wooded wonderland. Green and lush. Weathered park benches with magical gnomes hidden across the property. Oversized hammocks hanging from sturdy trees that touch the sky.

Something about the space connected us immediately to Mom. In fact, if I took a photo of my mother's property and a photo of Woodloch, you might not be able to tell the difference. Suddenly we were home and grounded.

Over the course of our time together, Alli and I packed every activity into every moment of the day. Woodloch is like a camp for grown-ups.

We took watercolor painting classes. We sharpened our pencils for a drawing class. We tie-dyed silk scarves. We painted tile coasters. And when we weren't crafting, we indulged in luxurious massages and facials. We spoiled ourselves rotten.

During our first dinner together, peering out into the wooded wonderland, holding hands, we toasted Mom. And we cried. Her presence in that moment was palpable. We both felt it.

We rested and played. Pampered ourselves. And added splashes of color back into our black-and-white world. We reconnected with each other in a sacred space.

I acknowledged that I was in active grief while also preparing for my father's death. He had battled Parkinson's disease for fifteen years. I had been a witness to the decline of my handsome and brilliant dad for more than a decade.

Snapshot. On September 19, 2019, 364 days after my mother's death, my dad passed away.

Life is ironic. For most of my childhood my dad served as the national president of Easterseals. He spent his life advocating for people with disabilities. As his disease progressed, his mobility decreased. His mind wandered. He began to hallucinate. Parkinson's is an ugly disease. His body was rigid. But when he hugged me, even at the end . . . it felt like he was still strong.

The worse his dementia got, the more he wanted to reminisce about the past. Pulling out the old slide projector and a box filled with slides brought him great joy. I learned more about him in the final months of his life by flipping through those slides in the rusty slide projector.

I was with him two weeks before his passing. I was able to hold his hand and talk to him about the journey he was about to take.

"I'm going to be gone for a long time, sweetie," he said.

And at that moment I felt I gave him permission to go. I left that day in August, knowing that I had just said goodbye to my dad.

When he died, I was prepared. I had watched him suffer. I had watched as people no longer treated him with the dignity and respect he had earned. He was no longer my dad.

In the span of 364 days, I had lost both my parents.

I was an orphan. A broken, exhausted, and raw shell of the woman I had been.

Snapshot. Six months later, our collective world changed. To me, Covid-19 felt like another loss in my life. I had restarted my business twice after losing my parents. Now, as the world shut down, I was terrified that I would not have the energy required to pivot . . . again. All I wanted to do was pick up the phone and call my mom. She had always been my greatest cheerleader. The stark reality of her being gone was overwhelming.

Navigating through this pandemic left me once again lost without a compass. Covid-19 was yet another stop on my grief journey.

I was unrooted. I wanted to run away from this new life that I had not chosen.

I knew I needed to return to a hammock in the woods. I knew that I needed to create the space for healing.

The woods called me back. And I listened. I returned to Woodloch.

I had never done anything like this. At fifty-eight years old, I had never checked into a hotel room alone.

The second visit provided me with the time I needed for myself. I refer to it fondly as #mymetreat.

A gravitational pull had brought me back to the sacred space. I had never considered myself to be a religious person, but I knew I was being drawn to this place again for a spiritual reason.

Upon arrival, I got my keys, dropped my bags on the floor of my room, and headed for the woods with my journal and camera in hand. I knew exactly where I needed to go. It was the hammock that Alli and I had discovered on our first visit.

I had forgotten that the forest was sprinkled with brass plaques inscribed with quotes.

Next to my hammock was a quote by Ralph Waldo Emerson. "Adopt the pace of nature: her secret is patience."

That was my sign.

Falling into that swing of connected fibers, I closed my eyes and just breathed.

I had initially resisted bringing my camera along on this journey, thinking it would interrupt my commitment to being "unplugged." Luckily, I had changed my mind and packed it in my bag. Because in that moment, I felt the need to capture the giant trees who had become my solace. I turned the camera on and removed the lens cap.

What I had forgotten was that the last picture I had taken was on the day I was closing on my mother's house. I had driven there to sit on the bench in the surrounding woods one last time. On my way down the driveway, I had paused to take a photo of the numbered house sign: 2670.

When I turned the camera to the On position at Woodloch and looked through the viewfinder . . . there it was, my sign. The photo of the house number I had taken months before.

I had also been resistant to bringing a journal. But someone I trusted had urged me to bring it along. In that moment on that hammock, I wrote like a wild woman. Words came flying onto the paper in a stream of consciousness. It was the release that I had needed but had not been ready for.

I allowed myself the space to leave my pain on the pages.

I don't know how long I stayed in the woods.

What I did know was that my heart and soul were coming back to life.

That afternoon, I returned to the place of pampering . . . the magical spa. This time, I was trying something new: a flotation tank.

A flotation tank is a sensory deprivation experience. The tank is pitch-black, lightproof, soundproof, and filled with water heated to the same temperature as the skin. The dissolved Epsom salt creates an anti-gravity effect. All of this creates an environment that allows you to float effortlessly on the surface of the water.

I was floating naked in a tank of salt water in a pitch-black room with an emergency cord at my side. The attendant had told me I could pull it if I decided this experience was not for me. And I was tempted.

I worked hard at getting comfortable. I tried using the pillow that they gave me to support my neck. That didn't work. I squiggled and squirmed around, fully aware of my awkwardness in this moment. I fought the ease of this experience by not letting go.

And then suddenly something shifted. I released my need to figure it out. I just closed my eyes and allowed my body to be still. To trust the water. And I was fully present in the moment. I had stopped fighting. I was experiencing a sense of peace in the letting go.

I decided to take a walk in the woods just before dusk, and took the path from the lodge toward a garden I was looking for. I was staying on the path and following the signs, but for some reason I stopped in my tracks. I was afraid. It was getting dark, and I was alone in the woods. I wasn't sure where I was going, but I decided to listen to my intuition. I turned around to walk back to the lodge.

I took three or four steps and then turned around again. Something inside me was telling me to move forward.

And that's when it happened. I heard rustling in the trees. With my camera in hand, I scanned the woods. Staring right at me was a beautiful female deer. We both stopped and looked at each other. Neither of us ran. Neither of us moved. We locked eyes. And she allowed me to take her picture. In that moment I was unequivocally certain that I was in the presence of my mother. And it was perfect.

Snapshot. I found my healing place.

When I headed home the next day, I knew that I had not run away from my life the day before. I wasn't escaping from my house and my husband. I was simply running toward a time of reconnection.

I keep that picture of the deer on my desk. Sometimes the sun hits it perfectly, and it's magic to me.

In May 2021, Alli and I returned to Woodloch. Instead of filling our schedule with activities, we leaned into the quiet and the peace of our sacred space.

We sought out the quiet nooks and crannies and the cozy couches. We turned down the noise from our first visit so that we could appreciate the stillness of the place.

And on this third visit, with my beautiful daughter at my side, we reconnected with my mother.

As a Mother's Day gift, Alli had found a medium for us to spend time with. If you've ever had this experience, you will know that entering this space comes with mixed emotions. There is unexplainable fear. Fear of not connecting to anyone. And fear of being disappointed in your lack of connection.

There we were. Sitting together on the end of the bed in our luxurious white spa robes with our computer on a pillow. Holding hands as the medium entered the Zoom room.

What happened in our time together with Marie, our medium, was nothing short of miraculous. My mom showed up in a big way that day.

I asked for clarity about what had happened the night of her accident. And I got it. I sought to understand what her eyes were telling me that horrific September morning. And I got it. Mom wanted us to know that we would be okay. Our intergenerational connection would endure. She would always be with us.

"She's so mad at herself for being so careless that night," Marie said. The scattered napkins had fallen from her hands as she'd gone downstairs to do a load of laundry that evening.

One of Mom's classic comments was "I know." It drove us crazy when she was alive. As the medium channeled the powerful force that was my mom's spirit, the words *I know* kept flying out of her mouth. Each story, each reference made me more certain that my mother was in the room.

All three of us got what we needed in that place that day. A chance to reconnect in a new way.

That afternoon, with my daughter at my side, I redefined my relationship with my mother. She gave me permission to let go of the snapshot that had haunted me, which allowed me to reframe it. It became abundantly clear that our three stars were reconnected. Shining brightly together.

In that moment, I was able to create a new snapshot. One in which I was serving as her guide for the next part of her journey. Her eyes were asking me for the help and support she had given me for fifty-six years.

This time together was taking us all on a journey of hope.

Getting to this moment had taken releasing the pain, the trauma, and the indescribable loss.

In the past three years, I have learned about the power of surrendering and letting go. I have stopped fighting the grief.

When I replace struggle with ease and grace, the lens through which I see my life changes.

"When the student is ready, the teacher will appear."

It might feel easier to run away from the snapshots that bring us pain. To stay busy. To be in constant motion. Because pain is raw and messy. Pain redefines us. Pain steals our best stuff.

What I have learned is that I can choose how I curate my story carousel. My 364-day grief journey will always be part of my story. Grief never becomes a well-healed scar. But it doesn't have to be an open wound.

There is divineness for me in still places with towering trees and bright green leaves. There is magic when you discover a gnome statue sitting cross-legged, meditating under a bench. Or a quote on a plaque next to your hammock in the woods that you know is there just for you.

The journey to find healing spaces has taken me from grief to gratitude. Gratitude for the life lessons my parents taught me. Gratitude for the friends and family who walked the grief journey alongside me. Grateful for the strength that I have accumulated over time through a series of heartbreaks. Grateful, knowing that the universe always has my back.

I have leaned into my intuition. I have trusted my gut. Each decision that I have made about pivots after loss has led me to personal growth and a reframing.

I have reclaimed my voice. I have stopped self-editing.

And, I have learned to think courageously.

There is something better on the other side of pain. I took my pain and pivoted my career to become a life coach, podcaster, storyteller, and curator of the Think Courageously community.

I have rearranged my slide show so that I can support other women on their journey to think courageously.

Snapshot. My office is now my sacred sanctuary. It is filled with photos of my mother and my daughter and the deer that locked eyes with me that day in the woods. A crescent moon mobile spins from a ceiling fan with three stars. And each morning when the light streams into the room, I know our constellation will be forever connected.

ABOUT THE AUTHOR

DEB CUMMINS STELLATO

Deb Cummins Stellato has always had a love affair with photography. For Deb, seeing the world through the lens of a camera is a daily occurrence. From the inspirational posters that covered her walls as a kid to the endless pet pics on her iPhone, photos have been the constant storytelling tool in Deb's life.

With the loss of both of her parents within a 364-day span, Deb had to redefine the snapshots of her life through a new lens: the beauty of sacred spaces. As the host of the Think Courageously podcast and as a journey coach, Deb supports women in creating their own safe spaces so that they can find the courage to make pivots.

Learn more about Deb at www.thethinkgoodcompany.com

Chapter 7

EMBRACE HEALING ADVENTURES

Becky Burroughs

"Whatever you are looking for is what you will find."

Grief

I am intimate with Grief. It crawls into bed with me late at night, burrowing under my covers and filling up every inch of my bed. Some nights, it lies so heavy on my chest, I cannot breathe.

In the beginning, I failed to respect its power, refusing to even acknowledge it by name, hoping that it would just go away. But Grief disguised as a bad mood will, instead, worm its way into the very marrow of your being, blow itself out of proportion, and bubble forth when you least expect it. It produces strange, even inquisitive looks and comments like, "Are you okay? You don't seem like yourself." Or from those who feel close enough to call it what it is, "You're kind of crabby."

In the past few years, Grief has pounded on my door several times in the form of death: the sudden death of my dad, the death of my forty-year marriage, the slow death of my mom, and the death of my job, all within a seven-year span. In the early days and months of Grief, it feels more like a violent takeover of the body, the mind, and every ounce of energy. This coup d'état called Grief storms in after a loss, accompanied by a myriad of feelings and emotions that deplete the hope of any normal functioning and leave one bone weary and numb.

Loss on top of loss stacks Grief on top of Grief, producing out-of-character responses that signal that you do not have the margin to manage it well. Looking back, I clearly see that I was depressed, overwhelmed with Grief, and not managing it well at all. I could not sleep and did not want to eat. During the day, I could feel hair graze my arms as it detached itself from my head to the point that my hairdresser noticed the hair loss. Unwelcome tears visited daily, sucking the life right out of me. Much like a house, boarded up in preparation for an impending hurricane, my tendency, when I am hurting, is to completely turn inward, so I wanted to be alone, even if it was not good for my mental health. I had no words, and when the situation necessitated that I form some, they came out in ways I did not intend. My garbled thoughts forgot things I typically do not forget. I made decisions I would not normally make. Sometimes, I had to remember to breathe.

To complicate matters, additional loss bubbled to the top to also be grieved: loss of identity and loss of the dream. I discovered new titles that were mine to wear. No longer anyone's wife, my new title was loaded with shame: divorced. My children were grown, with families of their own, so I wore a new title: extended family. Having no parents provided yet another title: orphan.

I work at a church, having left twenty-five years in education to embrace ministry, and I never looked back. I am mentally strong, or so I am told, but the elimination of my ministry role to help the bottom line tested my mental toughness even further. I did not have the margin to also grieve the loss of my position and its responsibilities, and the decreased compensation for my work. Even though I was immediately offered another ministry position at the same church, which I accepted, the story I told myself was that I had no value to anyone, and neither did my life's work. As I look at these words flowing from my fingers, they sound absurd, even to me. However, when one is drowning in the depths of despair from loss and Grief, they feel very, very real.

The only constant in my life, the only identity that remained, was child of God. I have loved God all of my life. My dad taught me early on that Jesus was the best friend I could ever have and that the Holy Spirit was a companion living in me and guiding me. That trifecta of love through this grieving process sustained me.

As part of my new identity, I developed new rituals. Every night, in the darkness and silence of my bedroom, I called out to God, much like on *The Waltons*, which I'd grown up watching, where they all called "good night" from the darkness of their bedrooms.

"I love you, God. I love you, Jesus. I love you, Holy Spirit" accompanied by three air high fives aimed toward heaven. This ritual comforts me still and reminds me that I am never alone.

Hope after loss comes only when one is willing to do the hard work of Grief. I continue to be a student of Grief and have a lot to learn from this masterful teacher, but this I know: Grief is a process with a purpose, and life after Grief can be beautiful, and meaningful, and in some ways, even better than before.

Fear

Married at the tender age of nineteen and alone for the first time in my life at the age of sixty, I had Grief and Fear firmly camped out in my home the day my husband walked out the door.

Fear followed me around every waking moment as I routinely checked doors and windows at night. Fear grabbed my arm and gasped whenever the doorbell rang. Sometimes Fear woke me in the middle of the night, convinced that it heard something that I needed to investigate. Out of habit, I would reach for the other side of the bed to nudge my husband, but no one was there, just Grief, who refused to be nudged. Fear and I would crawl out of bed and slink through the house, only to find the dogs sound asleep near the main entry. Deciding that if the dogs could sleep through the imaginary danger, so could we, Fear and I would head back to bed or move to the couch, turn on the TV, and wait out the night.

Fear was relentless. I feared being unloved and unlovable. I feared being alone for the rest of my life, never again to be enveloped in the arms of a man. I developed a fear of driving in the dark, a fear of a flat tire with no husband to call, and fear of car trouble as I traveled to visit grandchildren. I feared something breaking down in the house with no husband to fix it. I feared losing my job with no one to support me; I feared getting sick with no one to care for me. But the greatest fear of all, the one that thrust me into motion to get on with the hard work of grieving and therefore with the business of living my new life and creating a new dream, was this: the fear of becoming a bitter old woman.

I knew what she looked like, this bitter old woman, with her permanent scowl and piercing gaze. She repeatedly told her story to anyone willing to listen, and in her version, she was the victim. This trauma canceled her plans for the future, shattered her dreams, faded her hope, and threatened her very identity. Her life no longer had meaning or purpose. Her grumpy self robotically moved through each day, just waiting to die, and she died alone. I actually knew women like this, women whose lives stopped the day their husbands died or walked out the door, and this propelled me to action with one persistent thought:

As God is my witness, I will not be that woman.

The Road to Healing

The month of my fifty-ninth birthday was particularly lonely. One day, my son called. He was about to travel to several cities over the next few months to interview for a cardiology fellowship position, and he asked if I might like to go with him to one. This was a dream conversation, because if we are truthful here, when does a mom *ever* get to travel with her thirty-year-old married son? He would have preferred to take his wife, of course, but since it was the beginning of the school year and she was a teacher and coach, she could not take the time off. So he asked me.

"Of course I will go with you! Where?"

"Honolulu."

"Are you kidding me? Please do not joke with me about this. You are inviting me to go with you to Hawaii?"

"Yes, but we'll only be there for three days. I have an interview that will take about half a day, and the rest of the time we can explore the island."

The day we boarded the plane and took our seats, he turned to me.

"Mom, I think you're adventure deprived. So we're going to cram as much adventure as we can into this weekend."

I had never heard the term *adventure deprived* before, and to be honest, it stung a little. The truth often does. Nevertheless, I buckled up for the flight to Hawaii and, unbeknownst to me at the time, the road to healing.

In two and a half days, we rode Segways around Honolulu, parasailed a thousand feet over the Pacific Ocean, zip-lined at the North Shore, and snorkeled in Hanauma Bay. We crammed so much adventure into that weekend that I was pumped for days afterward.

I returned home with an epiphany: *I* am *adventure deprived*! *How did I not know this? What does it even mean?* It's not like I am a thrill seeker, although I surely enjoyed the thrills of that weekend.

For me it is more about the recognition that for too long I had been stuck, my feet in quicksand, my body lethargic and my brain in a fog. I knew this was expected, given that I was grieving, but I wanted more. If I was ever going to break through the hold Grief had on me, accompanied by the death grip of Fear, I needed to take a resilient approach to grieving. I also needed to see what would happen if I incorporated more fun, new, or interesting things into my life. Apparently I needed an adventure explosion to jump-start the process.

I vowed to myself to do sixty fun, new, or interesting things by my sixtieth birthday, which prompted the title for my new journal: 60 x 60. It was basically a numbered list of activities that I found to be fun, new, or interesting. The Hawaii adventure surely went in the journal, with each different event listed separately.

After returning home, I realized that *that* level of adventure is not sustainable, so my list also included things like going to a different restaurant, trying a new dish, reading an interesting book, and watching a good movie. My 60 x 60 quickly turned into 600 x 60 because of one amazing discovery: whatever you are looking for is what you will find. I was looking for a reason to get out of bed in the morning; I needed something to look forward to, something to talk about other than my pain. I needed the healing balm of laughter, and boy, did I find it!

My friends quickly jumped on board, each joking with the other that they wanted top billing in my journal. One friend and I went on a quest every Monday during lunch, looking for the best taco in Dallas, which led to the quest for the best cheeseburger and fries, and finally, the best fajitas. Eventually, I had to pull back on that or risk adding a new category: shopping for a new wardrobe.

On the week of my sixtieth birthday, having conquered 600 x 60, I went indoor skydiving with my son, one of my daughters, and their spouses. It was thrilling, and I thought at the time that it was just enough to satisfy my long-held desire to go skydiving. I told myself that indoor skydiving was the same thing, only safer. Little did I know that a few years later I would kick Fear out of a small prop plane, twelve thousand feet above the earth's surface, seconds before tumbling out myself, hands down my most exhilarating adventure to date.

My first Christmas season alone, I celebrated in a weird way that was oddly comforting. Beginning just after Halloween, I worked a Charles Wysocki jigsaw puzzle every night. His puzzles are always about home, family, and small town; I find them comforting. I did this while watching more than a hundred Hallmark movies that first Christmas season alone, living vicariously through the lives of the characters, assured that there would always be a happy ending. It was cathartic.

My grown children were instrumental to my healing, thoughtfully anticipating needs I might have, knowing that this first holiday season would be especially painful. One of my daughters, with the encouragement of her mother-in-law, enlisted the help of the others to make my first Christmas alone the best ever. This was the only Christmas I did not decorate or even put up a tree, and as December drew near, it became increasingly difficult to get into the holiday spirit. So, my precious children arranged for a package to be on my doorstep every day in December, leading up to Christmas. I became childlike, bounding out of bed each morning to see what would be on my doorstep. Each gift was thoughtfully chosen, each one just what I needed. It remains my most memorable Christmas yet.

My grandchildren are warm chocolate chip cookies, so full of love and affection. Every goodbye hurts my heart and usually requires the car trip home to shake it off. I love being Nana to my grandchildren. During this intense period of grieving, they seemed to instinctively know what I needed, so they did not withhold their gestures of love; they flowed freely.

My friends provided daily doses of healing. Calls to check on me, texts to remind me that I am loved, cards in the mail, and hugs without words were salve to my broken heart. Friends were present when I needed to talk and, on other days, sat with me in silence.

Joy

One week after my divorce was final, I went to New York City with a friend to attend a conference for women in ministry at a church in Manhattan. Still reeling from the death of life as I knew it, I felt that this combination business and pleasure trip might be good for me. We extended the trip long enough to do the touristy things. But the most important entry into my journal that week referenced a short conversation that changed my life.

On this particular day, the speaker, a college professor from a Christian university, had an encouraging message for this group of women. I remember enjoying her presentation. What I do not remember is one word she said.

I felt connected to her, even though we had never met. Shared trauma often does that, and we were both members of a club we'd never asked to join: women who found themselves divorced after decades of marriage. This club has a secret language. Its reluctant members can communicate with knowing looks and ironically finish each other's sentences like lifelong friends because of a shared experience with pain.

After her presentation, as women were milling around, I mustered up all of my Courage and approached her. I introduced myself, thanked her for her presentation, and with tears puddling in my eyes, blurted out my reason for approaching her. I mumbled something about my recent divorce and the knowledge that it was something we had in common.

She grabbed me by the shoulders, looked deep into my eyes, and said, "Becky, after my divorce, I vowed that every day I would do at least *one* thing that brings me Joy, even if it is just driving through the Dairy Queen to get a Blizzard." In the midst of her Grief, she chose Joy.

The journey of Grief contains multiple forks in the road, requiring choice. One choice, nestled inside of my comfort zone, lures with its downhill slope and familiar path. The end of this road is unclear, and its impending potholes and roadblocks are not immediately apparent but lurk under the surface. Although the journey of Grief always begins on this road, getting stuck in the muddy sadness or spiraling down in the pothole of depression extends and complicates the journey of grief, interfering with healing.

Another choice that appears at various points along the journey looks to be uphill and exists outside of my comfort zone. It feels riskier, with its uneven terrain and unfamiliar landmarks. However, this path provides surprising twists and turns, revelations, and new experiences. This path is the healing path where resilience is strengthened; at the end awaits a new identity nestled in Hope.

The words of this sweet woman confirmed that at some point I had chosen the path of healing, and propelled me to set my next bodacious goal: 7000 x 70. Why not? By this time, I was a master at finding the fun, the new, or the interesting in the smallest of things, and Joy has become one of my favorite words.

We often interchange the words *Joy* and *Happy*. I want to be Happy and even search for things, people, and experiences that will make me Happy. I have even heard people justify decisions by saying, "God wants me to be Happy," but I have been unable to find evidence in scripture that this is true. What I have found are numerous references to Joy, seeking, finding, and actually deciding to be joyful, even in the midst of trials and suffering. The quest for happiness is elusive, since it seems to depend on what's happening. Do you feel good? Are things going your way? Did you get what you wanted? Did you achieve your goals? The answers to these questions are pivotal to receiving a visit from this fickle friend called Happy. But once things go south, Happy vanishes.

In my search for Joy, Grief tagged along and demanded my full attention at night when I was alone. But when the endless night gave way to the dawn of a new day, I left Grief behind to wallow on its own, and flung myself into the arms of Joy. Joy does not smother me like Grief does, with its ever-present dark cloud. Joy nestles in my heart like a timid child playing hide-and-seek, holding its breath, waiting to hear when it is safe to come out. Poised to travel from my heart to my mind to my words, and to permeate every aspect of my day, all Joy needs to hear from me is Gratitude. So, I begin the day cataloging each thing for which I am grateful until I can feel Joy oozing through my system.

That is why I prefer Joy to happiness. Joy comes from within; it is a decision, a state of mind, and the secret ingredient of Joy is Gratitude. So, rather than listing things that make me Happy, I focus on listing those things for which I am grateful, because I am seeking Joy. It is also a double dip. I get to experience Joy in the moment and again later, when I read about it in my journal.

Courage
When you lose your identity after compounding loss, the path is cleared for finding a new one, or, better yet, discovering who you were all along. When you are married, the two become one, compromises are made, deals are

struck, and we language is used. *We* like to eat at this restaurant. *We* go to these places for vacation. For the holidays, *we* have these traditions.

When *we* becomes *I*, it is vital to the healing process for you to decide—or in some cases, learn—what *I* want to do. I began to think about restaurants *I* like or want to try. I decided how *I* wanted to spend my weekend, and with whom. I love to travel, a pastime my former husband didn't share, so my brain began churning with all the places I wanted to go.

I had always wanted to learn Spanish. I took Spanish lessons online, and six months later, when I was given a four-week sabbatical, I knew with certainty how I needed to spend that time. I packed my bag and boarded a plane for Puerto Vallarta in Jalisco, Mexico, to attend a Spanish immersion school and delve more deeply into this beautiful language. I knew that Fear would be my traveling companion, which was fine by me, because Fear needed to learn a thing or two about my new identity and the limited role I would allow it to play in my life moving forward.

For four weeks, Fear was put to the test. I lived with a woman who spoke no English, and we communicated with the help of Google Translate. She lived in the Marina section of Puerto Vallarta, which required that I ride a city bus for thirty minutes each day to school. I had to learn how to navigate the bus system in Spanish, including how and when to get from the bus stop to school on foot and back again. More than once I got on the wrong bus, only to bail, walk for miles, and find a bus that would take me home. The buses were not air-conditioned and were grossly overcrowded, with every seat taken and people packed into the aisle, gripping the bar overhead and jostling together with each shift of the gears. My preference was to stand and be jostled rather than sit and sport a sweat ring on my shorts for the rest of the day.

I learned to shop at the local stores, to negotiate pricing when appropriate, and to pay in cash. I learned simple conversational Spanish, ate Mexican food every day, and made new friends. The most important thing I learned was that Fear can have a death grip on me only if I allow it.

Fear lives on the borders of my comfort zone. Whenever I step near the border, to try something new or different, Fear stands in the way, whispering—even shouting if necessary—words designed to keep me small, safe, insignificant, and most of all, fearful. When I shrink back, Fear has done its job and takes a rest until the next time it is needed.

Choosing the path outside my comfort zone tests my Courage and puts Fear in its place, no longer allowing it to rule my life. All the magic happens along this path.

The four weeks I spent in Mexico were pivotal to my healing; a ton of Courage was required. Every time I stepped outside my comfort zone, more Courage was built, like muscles put to the test by barbells. Step after step outside my comfort zone expanded its borders, putting Fear further and further away and shrinking its hold on me.

I left a piece of my heart in Puerto Vallarta when I left four weeks later, for it was there that Fear and I reached an understanding. No longer would Fear be allowed to rule my life. My new identity included Courage. With my newfound Courage put to the test, alone in another country, my mantra became

It's okay to feel the Fear. But we are going to do this thing anyway, even if we have to do it scared.

That is Courage at its finest. I often think of the difference between being Brave and having Courage. There are many things I am Brave about doing, usually because I have the experience, education, or expertise to do them. When I am Brave, I have no fear. In contrast, Courage accepts the presence of Fear but moves forward anyway.
When I came to grips with this dichotomy, I realized that because of the invasive presence of Fear my entire life, an important aspect of my new identity needed to include Courage. I also realized that strengthening my Courage and becoming more resilient begins with continued, persistent steps outside of my comfort zone.

I returned to PV a year later, this time for two weeks, to once again attend Spanish immersion school. My host had become my friend, and she said I was welcome to stay in her home, even though she would be out of town. She returned a couple of days before my return to the States, and we went to dinner the last night, conversing in Spanish throughout our meal at an Italian restaurant overlooking the marina. She was also a member of the club—women who found themselves divorced after decades of marriage—so we spoke the secret language of the club, only this time, in Spanish.

Hygge

Divorced for less than a year, a friend who knew I was entertaining the thought of a tattoo asked if I would go with her to get one to celebrate her milestone fortieth birthday. Without thinking it through, I immediately responded, "Yes!" Yet, my search for the perfect image to have emblazoned on my wrist proved fruitless. I have small wrists, and the pictures I liked were too large. But the real problem was that I am a words person. I love words, the way they feel in my mouth, the way they sound on my tongue. I love looking up word meanings and even their origins. I am a certified word nerd. On my phone are screenshots of words and their definitions; I have it bad. So, I shifted to a word search and began looking for one word that meant "doing at least one thing every day that brings me Joy." I could not find such a word in the English language, but I did in other languages. I chose the word used by the Danes: *hygge*.

In Denmark, it is dark twenty-four hours a day one month of the year, which seems to bring on high incidences of depression and suicide. So, the Danes invented the concept of hygge (pronounced hue-gah). It is the Danish ritual of enjoying life's simple pleasures and includes elements such as a warm fireplace, a comfy chair, a cozy blanket, a hot drink or glass of wine, a good book, comfort food, soft lighting, a scented candle, perhaps good friends and soft music.

After learning about hygge, I immediately purchased hygge books and games, with a desire to learn everything I could about this magical ritual. I knew that this was the word that I wanted permanently etched on my wrist. I showed the word to the tattoo artist, and said I wanted the word facing me.

His response: "When you tattoo a word, it is customary to have it face outward so others can read it."

I shook my head firmly. "Nope. I want it to face me. I need the daily reminder to find at least one thing every day that brings me Joy."

As previously mentioned, I have small wrists, meaning there is absolutely no fat on them; it's a genetic thing. When the tattoo artist turned on his tool and touched my skin, it felt like my wrist bone was being jackhammered. Next to multiple childbirths without anesthesia, this was, by far, the most physically painful thing I have ever experienced. In addition to crying, I was Lamaze-breathing while my friend held my hand and rubbed my back. Five minutes later, the tattoo artist turned off his tool and the room went silent; my pain immediately stopped.

Oh, if only emotional pain could be turned off so quickly.

Around that time, I enrolled in Divorce Recovery at a local church. On the first night, the leader said, "We recommend that you wait at least one year for every ten years you were married to begin dating. The reason we say that is that we cannot talk you into waiting two."

At the time I thought, *Forty years. That means I have to wait four to eight years before I start dating. That is a long time of loneliness; it's a lifetime!*

But now, looking back, I see the wisdom in that advice, because the last thing on earth I needed to do to heal was quickly find another man. I have now been divorced four years. I can see that any man who would have been attracted to me when I was at my most vulnerable would not be a man I would be attracted to after I did the hard work of Grief. My journey of Grief has been a wild, courageous ride of learning and adventure, dreaming and hope. I am still buckled up for the ride.

Grief will not be ignored. Its process must be followed and its purpose respected. At some point you will find yourself at the fork in the road, torn between the familiar path of Grief upon Grief that has you feeling stuck, or spiraling out of control, and the other path that has you firmly outside of your comfort zone.

If you are ready in the grieving process to explore the woman God created you to be and you want to find her, I urge you to draw upon every ounce of Courage you can muster and take that first, courageous step. Choose the path of healing.

My quest to find my true identity also has me on another career path. I became a certified life and leadership coach so that I can help other women navigate life's transitions.

Around the time of my divorce, I had counseling to work through the trauma, and desperately needed it. However, there came a point when I was ready for forward movement. I wanted to discover my true identity; I needed hope and really wanted someone to help me with that, but at the time, did not know what coaching was or how it could benefit me.

A coach does not take the place of a supportive network of family and friends, or a counselor. It also does not replace the love of a church family. But here's the hard truth: those who love you will actively support you for a time and then return to their normal lives, long before you are far enough along in the grieving process or even ready to let go of their support. That's just the way it works.

So, if you need support and guidance at the point where you are ready to dream about your new life instead of dwelling on your old one, consider hiring a coach who will walk those steps with you, guiding and encouraging you along the way.

I have learned much from this masterful teacher, Grief. Choosing the scary path, the one that took me out of my comfort zone and expanded my Courage, moved me beyond grieving to resilient grieving. Once again, I am filled with Hope, having done the hard work of Grief. I am living a rich, full, adventurous life, finding the Joy in every day, and dreaming about the future.

I have found hygge.

ABOUT THE AUTHOR

BECKY BURROUGHS

Becky Burroughs spent most of her life setting high expectations, driving herself into the ground, denying her feelings, and hiding her fears. It took a series of traumatic events, and a full-blown identity crisis, for her to discover her true self and to love herself as God loves her—unconditionally.

Always a champion for others, Becky is now a life and leadership coach for Christian women, a speaker, and an author, encouraging and empowering women to find their true identity, know their worth, and use their voice.

When she is not with her grandchildren, she can be found jumping out of perfectly good planes or traveling the world.

Becky would love to connect with you via Becky Burroughs Coaching (on Facebook and Instagram). Or visit her website, www.beckyburroughs.com

Chapter 8

BUILD THE LIFE YOU NEED

Marie Masse

"Your stories are guides to who you are and who you want to become."

It's not supposed to be this way. After all we've done to get here—two immigrations, five moves, all the times he's paid off my credit cards, babies, new job, new house, new everything—what kind of wife would I be to say, "Never mind," and pull the rug out from under him? Flirting with the idea of a different life was a betrayal to the vision we'd woven together . . . but my commitment was fading. I'd awakened to a life that wasn't made for who I was becoming.

With a history of failures, changing my mind, and debt, this was a scary and embarrassing realization. *It's not supposed to be this way? Then how's my life "supposed" to be?*

We had a great life already, and yet I felt this deep void. I couldn't even name it, so I made excuses. . . . *It's just the season we're in. This too shall pass. Dave has contributed to my dreams and wants before his own more times than I can count. What's wrong with me? We've already come so far. Changing it up is selfish. With all I have, how ridiculously privileged am I to desire something different? Shame on me! I need to work on my gratitude and contentment.* The more I tried to ignore it, the more "it's not supposed to be this way" called in relentless waves.

> I had everything I could possibly want—yet I was failing to appreciate it.
> — Gretchen Rubin, The Happiness Project

> I had actively participated in every moment of the creation of this life—so why did I feel like none of it resembled me?
> — Elizabeth Gilbert, Eat, Pray, Love

> I'm a free spirit who never had the balls to be free.
> — Cheryl Strayed, Wild

I'm not the first woman to arrive here. Gretchen, Elizabeth, and Cheryl are just a few of the women (with millions of book sales each!) who have taken notice of their lives and been haunted by the view. Perhaps they were even more haunted because they knew they had led themselves there—that kind of responsibility and ownership is hard to swallow.

Elizabeth Gilbert spent a year abroad, immersed in spiritual and personal exploration. Gretchen Rubin extensively researched happiness, and mapped out and executed her yearlong Happiness Project. Cheryl Strayed purchased a Pacific Crest Trail guidebook and a pair of boots, and (having never backpacked before) left to walk the PCT for ninety-four days alone.

How many times have you romanticized a soul-searching adventure of your own? Wished to push Pause and take uninterrupted time to name a void, face a fear, resolve a problem, heal from anguish, or figure out who you are and what you want for your life?

If you've heard "it's not supposed to be this way," how have you responded? Do you ignore the call and persevere with the grit and will of a woman? If so, is it possible that your perseverance is a mask to quiet your disappointment of settling (i.e., believing, "This is how it is. I will stay strong and live out this life I've committed to, because that's life... *That's what you do.*")?

We see those women as brave and admirable, because they took a stand. Each in her own way, those women (re)connected with who they are and the story line they wanted to live. They sought out healing and did the work. They redefined their version of a good life—better aligned with who they're becoming. They ended their journeys with the self-love, self-trust, and self-actualization necessary to grow a well-nourished life. Using my stories, I found that for myself, too.

My "it's not supposed to be this way" calls grew noticeable in 2016. I was restless, and it made no sense. I had everything:

- Dave and I were six years into our solid marriage—and still in love.
- We had two healthy kids: Kendall (four and a half) and Levi (two and a half).
- We lived on a rural dirt road in a 3,200-square-foot dream home on two acres.
- The kids went to a Blue Ribbon School and day care only three minutes down the road.
- Dave had a secure, "good money" job with benefits.
- I was immersed in a business I loved.
- A biweekly cleaning service made our home sparkle.
- We saw our families once a month or so, as well as for holidays and birthdays.

What more could I want? I was living a perfect, highly privileged life, checking all the boxes, only to be taunted by this baffling void within. *It's not supposed to be like this.* What spurred me into facing it was our son.

The road with Levi has been rough. His arrival, five weeks premature, came with a simultaneous hysterectomy for me, and he was two years old before he slept through the night. Several months into a good sleep rhythm, we thought parenting was about to get easier. . . . How wrong we were!

For over a year up to this point, Dave had worked twelve-hour night shifts: 5:00 p.m. to 5:00 a.m., five days a week, and some weekends. As awful as the schedule sounds, it gave us more time for him to co-parent than if he worked days. Plus, Dave made our mornings smooth and drove the kids to childcare for me—a godsend on cold Michigan winter mornings! The night routine, however, was all Momma.

Bedtime was treasured. Kendall did something quiet. Levi and I went upstairs, to his bedroom, and rocked in the overpriced (but I'd just have to have it) nursery chair. Snuggling him with his favorite blanket, I sang to him while rubbing and patting his back. When he was nearly asleep, I laid him in bed and he soothed himself to sleep. The whole routine took only twenty minutes or so.

In April 2016, we went on our first family vacation. When we got home from that trip, Levi (now two and a half) was *different*. There's much to share on this, but the hardest part—and what sent me over the edge—was bedtime. It became a two-hour affair! He came out of his room a hundred times. I practiced "don't engage or say a word" and put him right back in his bed. Next, I tried teaching him to at least stay in his room doing quiet things. He came out laughing within five minutes. I said, "Screw it," and test-drove a later bedtime . . . except Levi couldn't stay up and be chill. He was vibrant and pure wild! Ignoring the behavior only led to him finding new ways to provoke us. He broke or threw things like toys or our lamp. He often hurt his sister by biting, hitting, or throwing things at her. Levi defined hyper.

Listen, I'm no fool. We had a quiet, calm routine that began a couple of hours before bedtime. I did my best to get him exhausted and worn out. I watched his sugar intake, artificial food dyes, and screen time. *Nothing helped.*

I even tried having Kendall go to bed first. Levi didn't do "quiet play" such as with toddler blocks, wood puzzles, or coloring, and wanted to be in whatever room I was in. His high energy and volume made it *impossible* to read to, snuggle with, and love on Kendall. She'd either get mad . . . or join the wild.

The childcare center had a growing list of complaints about Levi's behavior too. After attempts to reason with him, be consistent in discipline (aka frighten him into submission), praise him, lower my voice (so he'd be calm enough to hear me), redirect, and whatever other advice I'd been given, "it's not supposed to be this way" screamed on a whole other level. I took Levi to his pediatrician for a behavior consultation.

"He's still so young," Dr. B. said. "Get him a mini-trampoline and a soccer net to get some of that energy out. He's just wild and all boy. If he's roaming around at night, put a child safety lock on his door, because that's dangerous." We tried it all, but the bedtime games held strong, night after night.

Everything made sense a few years later when Levi received a diagnosis of attention deficit hyperactivity disorder and oppositional defiant disorder (ADHD and ODD). Parenting a neurodivergent mind—with an emphasis on intense hyperactivity, impulsivity, and the games of an ODD master— is all-consuming and fragile. Everyday feels like diffusing a bomb, moment to moment, without all the right tools. Unknowingly parenting a toddler who hasn't received a diagnosis—especially after the doctor you trust dismisses your concerns—while flying solo (when Dave worked)? I have no words.

One night, Kendall was set up with the TV and I went upstairs for Levi's bedtime. My tipping point happened when I came back down and noticed that she was watching a different movie. The girl had successfully rented a movie off Amazon Prime! *It's not supposed to be like this.* My momma heart broke for how much she was alone while I was with Levi.

Soon after that, my anguish erupted. All it took was a single glance. It was an ordinary weekday with the kids at home (no childcare). Nothing noteworthy had happened. As on any other day, Dave started getting ready for work in the midafternoon. I was by the hallway, and he was standing at the kitchen counter. Noticing him putting together his lunch gave me an overwhelming jolt.

It's not supposed to be like this.
It's not supposed to be like this.
It's not supposed to be like this.

The thought of him leaving me alone with the kids . . .
again . . . destroyed my grit with overwhelming despair.
God, please, I don't want him to go. I can't do this.

I stepped into the living room to catch my breath. I was
a doe in headlights. I couldn't move or say a word. I
zoned out in panic, and no one noticed my unstoppable
unraveling. *He's only going to work, for heaven's sake!
Hold it together!*

Moments later, Dave made his afternoon rounds (always
to the kids first) for hugs, kisses, and goodbye. When
he came in for my turn, I lost it. Standing in the living
room, I fell into Dave, fell apart, and begged him to do
something. *Anything.* I needed help. I needed change for
our family. When he remained calm, every cell in my body
refused to surrender.

"You don't get it! I'm telling you, I am broken. Why aren't
you reacting? Isn't it dangerous to leave your kids with
this mental case?" I wanted to see him crumble and
cry and panic too. I wanted to know he understood the
seriousness of what I was feeling. I wanted to know I
wasn't alone. Then he did what he does: he held me as if
to take my pain and worry for himself. Sobbing in his arms
reminded me: we're in this together. I returned to my
center, and he was late for work.

Dave brought home news of relief the very next morning.
God, I love that man. Luckily, his boss was a family guy and

said Dave could come into work once the kids were in bed. Hallelujah! However, knowing this was only a temporary solution for the summer, my restlessness grew.

Coming from middle-class grandparents, aunts and uncles, and my own parents being 9-to-5 wage earners, I didn't know a different way of life. All through school, I believed what we're fed: *get good grades, get into a good college, and you'll get a good job.*

Now, with a bigger view of various lifestyles and urgency in my soul, I was open to radical risks if it meant Dave could be with us. Togetherness was top of mind. I was determined to shape this hard season into a wildly better life.

At the time, I was a documentary family photographer and owned an educational website for photographers. My theory was that I'd continue to photograph stories for clients and work with photographers on their stories and marketing. All I needed was my laptop and a hotspot so I could get a wireless internet connection. If it didn't work out, we could always return to the lifestyle we knew. So, I tossed my idea to Dave. "What if we sell everything, 'retire' you, and road-school the kids from a camper while I keep working from around the country?"

My friend Eboni says she notices how fast I make decisions and take action. I agree (even more so the older I get), but you should know I wasn't born with innate courage or resilience. I've grown my self-trust and shed fear around failure through failing . . . *a lot*!

Vulnerability with men before Dave? Shameful. Working in mortgage sales? A failure that resulted in a bankruptcy and foreclosure at twenty-three. Living in another country while recovering from said bankruptcy and foreclosure? Busted by immigration. My attempt at a lucrative photography career by posing families into superficial "love and laughter" portraits (before discovering a real life, documentary approach)? Fail.

Debt again after bankruptcy? Yup. Hid car from the repo man? Oh yes, I did! Medicaid attempted to recall coverage after my daughter was born? Total nightmare. Yelled at and spanked my son for his behavior? Still cringing over the mom I used to be. I was even mean to a friend the last time I saw her . . . *and then she died.*

Failure is only a redirect and an opportunity to be better. So, why not be more brazen? We drove five hours into Canada and purchased a 1970 Airstream Ambassador for less than two thousand dollars. Our intention was to gut it and rebuild.

Each piece we ripped out of the Airstream represented one step closer to being untethered and together. *Our life is coming together, for real this time. "It's not supposed to be this way" will stop taunting me. Come summer 2017, we'll be on the road and really living*!

The Airstream project progressed through fall, then came to a sudden halt when some parts we needed were unavailable. We tarped our Airstream and closed out 2016. *Screw you and your happiness project, Gretchen.* All I could see was what wasn't working, and it seemed the more I chased my happiness, the more noise I caught instead.

During my Airstream plan, I hadn't met my self-actualization yet. After working with a couple of mentors early in 2017, everything *actually* started to shift in a "mostly Marie" direction. Let me explain. . . .

For five years, I'd been making the kind of photography I treasure most: recognizable and highly meaningful stories. One reason this matters comes from having made the photo board displays for my grandpa's funeral. Seeing his younger self in pictures was awesome, and also saddening. There were no photographs of the grandpa in *my* memories.

There were no photos of him tending to his garden, reading the newspaper in his chair at their breakfast nook in the morning, or on the couch when he'd fallen asleep to Jay Leno. Those familiar scenes are what I value in a photograph. With the heart of a story-centric photographer, I've grown hyper-aware of my most meaningful stories.

On my first call with my new mentor, Nikki, I carried
on about why my photography approach is amazing.
She captured my words on our call notes: "I could talk
about this forever!" Seeing them through her eyes is
when *I got it*. . . . Nikki taught me how to notice and
lean into my own insights.

My next mentor, Suze, showed me how to see myself
in others. The things that trigger you, and that you
admire in others, are always a reflection of yourself
and the meanings you've given certain behaviors.
Through this practice, I saw more depth in who I
am. Suze also reconnected me with Little Marie and
taught me to see Future Marie.

Those mentorships expanded how I see personal stories.
Consider these stories that have inspired me. . . .

We called my maternal grandparents Papa Bob and
"Cracker." Cracker was short for Graham Cracker, a
nickname one of my cousins gave her. I used to go to
their house to spend one night . . . which often became
four. I loved my time there. Cracker and I made fireworks
on shirts with puffy fabric paint, she taught me to
crochet, we watered her gardens together (where I fell
in love with her rock collection), and one year we started
a postcard collection. After *All My Children*, Cracker
napped, and I'd sneak into the kitchen for an Archway
molasses cookie or two. After *Oprah* came on, Papa Bob
got home from work. He'd let me play on his computer

in his Joe Camel-scented office, went for walks with me, and taught me a little about drawing.

Cracker helped me host the fancy tea party I'd been wanting to have for years—complete with guests (her neighbor and my aunt), tea sandwiches, and the best part: her real china. That was also the summer she visited our family cabin for the first time . . . unaware it would also be her last.

My childhood overflowed with stories like these.

At our suburban home, I spent many afternoons up a tree. I tossed a rope over a branch to pull up things to do, snacks, and a drink in a five-gallon bucket. From the biggest apple tree in our backyard, I reveled in my own world.

Holidays were always the same: spent with extended family and good food. I went out for "dinner and a show" nights with my mom and great-grandmother JoJo. Dad's annual hunting trip meant a fun hotel weekend with Mom. Every third Sunday in July was the Zywicki family reunion.

Up north at the family cabin, I lived for dawns spent fishing with my dad, accompanying him on slow drives along Hamilton Road looking for deer, and hiking to "the bowl," a deep, rounded hollow in the forest that looked like it had been created with an ice cream scoop years ago. Back home in the suburbs, weekends were opportunities for us to make the hour drive to Lapeer, Michigan, and the surrounding areas. We'd cruise through the nature-heavy, rural landscape, look at homes for sale, and dream of a life outside of the city and suburbs.

My uncle Steve lived in the forest and had a pond. My sister, Amanda, and I spent hours there catching enormous bullfrogs. Up north at the family cabin, she and I hopped from mound to mound of knee-high, grass-covered dirt clumps along the lake to see how far out we could go. We caught painted turtles together . . . and got caught by a beehive once too.

When Uncle Ken, Aunt Linda, and my cousin Jamie came up to the cabin, falling asleep was to the sound of adults playing euchre (a card game) around the table. Jamie and I spent our summer days on four-wheelers. We all went on long snowmobile trips in winter.

My paternal grandparents, Papa Stan and Grandma Louise, also had an "up north" where I counted wild turkeys in the field every morning, picked up their fallen feathers, and ate lunch at a picnic table beneath the birch trees. All of us kids splashed and caught crayfish in the creek.

I could carry on with stories made with many more important people, but do you get my point? Your tiny stories make your value words *mean* something. When you think *values*, you probably think *family*, *health*, *marriage*, and so on. Those words, however, are *categories* lacking an emotional charge. You feel a charge of emotion when you connect with your specific tiny stories that embody each value category.

The stories I mentioned above are highly meaningful to me. Well, they say all good things come to an end . . . and all of those times have ended for me. I spoke about this at a conference once. Afterward, an attendee shared that she understood, because of her own story. "It feels like I've been robbed," she said. That's exactly it. I fear a future day when I notice more ended stories and feel like I missed them.

An obvious treasure of mine: the family cabin up north. When I think about the cabin, my brain defaults to what I miss in tiny story format: "the bowl" we hiked to, the raccoons we saw, starry nights on the dock, and more. Can you spot what's missing? I'd overlooked *how I felt* in the stories.

The thread in my stories was clear: I felt high levels of aliveness and meaningfulness when living out those stories. That was it! My emotional energy within my most treasured stories was the void I couldn't name.

Your stories are more than warm memories. If you allow them, your stories are guides to who you are and who you want to become. Insider secret: This is why you don't have to run off to Bali, start a Happiness Project, or take to the wild.

When I looked at my current life, I realized I was spending most days in a state of waiting and restlessness—rarely having moments of aliveness and meaningfulness. I believed in the same ol' lie many people deny: "Yes, I'm living on purpose." Wrong.

Think about it: You don't want to see yourself as living in survival mode, having settled for the status quo, or as wasting your most precious limited resource—time. No! You want to be in the driver's seat of your life. You want to see yourself as *living with intention*. You're living *on purpose* for what matters most, right? Well, let me tell you about those sneaky buzzwords. . . .

They're promoted as if to say, "If you're living with intention and living on purpose, then you're on your way to living your 'best, most fulfilled life.'" The fine print for that promo, however, gets overpowered by our desire to believe that we're on the right track, because that tells our ego we're safe.

The fine print reads, "Results may vary. These phrases may act as a placebo for an underlying truth: you're denying your own void or ignoring the 'it's not supposed to be this way' call."

Making many choices through the years told me *I'm intentional.* In reality, the only choices I saw to make were like ordering a modern culture-centric life in a box.

Things like this:

- courthouse marriage or wedding ceremony?
- suburban life or rural?
- hardwood or laminate?
- 9-to-5 or stay-at-home mom?
- public school or private?

For more than fifteen years I'd lived on purpose—growing a "good life." Except, it wasn't *my* good life. I ran toward whatever gave the least resistance and the most opportunities . . . never what was uniquely "Marie" and enlivening. I chased an ideal life as defined by beliefs I'd internalized through generational, cultural, and societal conditioning.

You can *feel* intentional and on purpose for your life . . . and still completely miss your best, most fulfilled life.

When I revisited how we could change our lifestyle, I realized that most urgent was the need to stop feeling like we were in an endless state of waiting—for bedtime, for the weekend, for summer, for the next family vacation, and so on. Long Michigan winters, two kids under five—one with undiagnosed ADHD, remember—and Dave's long work hours were my biggest sources of stress. The long hours and high-stress aerospace job weighed on Dave too—especially when he was coming home to a grumpy wife and another job: parenting. As a family, we felt the most aliveness and meaningfulness up north, at the family cabin. *Well, cabin life is for escape and play, not day-to-day living. Or could it be?*

I ran this insight and four options by Dave: (1) stay here, do nothing, and ride it out; (2) stick with the original Airstream plan; (3) sell everything first, find a move-in-ready camper, and go ASAP; (4) move somewhere up north to live in my beloved forest. Well, moving up north was quickly off the table, because . . . *even longer winters.* As we ruled out option four, an idea struck. We could nix the camper-travel life and move somewhere warmer and abundant with "cabin vibes."

We didn't make any decisions that night. Within days, in May 2017, Dave said, "A guy at work said Greenville, South Carolina, is great."

I responded, "Never heard of it," and promptly planned a trip south. We booked a mountaintop Airbnb home in Zirconia, North Carolina, because why not give this scouting trip a vacation vibe?

In July, we packed the kids, a stack of Dave's resumes (each with my handwritten note "in town for in-person interviews now through 7/27"), and a list of potential workplaces. We drove twelve hours south with zero expectations or attachment to any kind of outcome. *Doing* something—besides waiting for life to change— was enough for me.

We dropped off Dave's resumes—whether the place was hiring or not—all around the unfamiliar city and surrounding cities. I was chief navigator. The kids spent the week on iPads in the back seat. We squeezed in playground picnics in the southern summer heat by day and grilled delicious meals in the mountains by night.

We saw rhododendrons, took the kids to waterfalls, and heard katydids sing at night—all firsts for us. It felt like up north, but more amplified—*more wild*.

One week and 2,500 miles later, we were back home in Michigan. Dave accepted a job offer, and everything moved fast after that. About six weeks later, we landed at a rental home in South Carolina. The home was delightful and only four minutes from Dave's new workplace. However, the corner lot and the neighborhood quickly became sources of stress. *It's not supposed to be this way . . . again, already?*

We'd said we wouldn't jump into buying a house until we got to know the area, but we didn't even last a month. The second house we viewed became our home just after Christmas 2017.

I never imagined where speaking up about my "it's not supposed to be this way" shame would take us. I figured we'd land in a suburb, but at least we'd be in a warmer place and have more time together. Instead, we found our own little mountain . . . Masse Mountain. My mind is still blown.

One morning, early in May 2018, I set up a bistro table and chair on my new driveway. *Pinch me. Do I really get to work outside this early in the year?* The air was warm, the sun was bright, and the green of the forest surrounded me. My senses were enlivened. *Wow.* I was captivated and felt a nudge to notice my life.

I'd experienced a moment like this before. . . . Looking around at our life and home in Michigan, I thought I'd felt genuine gratitude. Now I see I'd felt only "should" gratitude. "Should" gratitude is palpable, but it's more like a high-five. You believe you're on track to fulfill the life you *should* be living.

"Each one of us has a prototype of how we were taught subconsciously to receive love, to receive validation, to receive worth and many of us mold to that very quickly," says Dr. Shefali Tsabary, a clinical psychologist. In shaping my life to fit the image, or prototype, I was attached to, like many of us unknowingly do, I'd lost connection with my essence. Therefore, I'd had no idea that a higher measure of gratitude even existed . . . or that it's available for all of us (*including you*) when we stop trying to shape our essence to fit the images we've adopted.

So, this new moment was different. I noticed a little green anole (a tiny lizard) hurrying across my new driveway. My heart leaped just like it did when Little Marie spotted deer on Hamilton Road with my family. Just like the little girl who fearlessly explored the woods up north and spent afternoons up in the apple tree. I recognized my state of being: I felt alive. With that, I met gratitude at a new depth. This gratitude was spiritual, not surface level, and moved through my core about as subtly as a drum solo. It was incredible.

This move to South Carolina was a homecoming to a wildly *right* life for us. I finally understand the "it's not supposed to be this way" call in a way I didn't before, because now I can see: *this is how it's supposed to be.*

Four years in, I'm in a life that kindles the best version of who I want to become . . . and that kindles my story line daily (not only in pauses for vacation or on the odd nights we grab a pizza). Aliveness and meaningfulness regularly surge through me, like when I'm . . .

- noticing views in new seasons;
- spotting wildlife, discovering strange bugs, and hearing unfamiliar birds;
- calling the coyotes with Kendall and hearing them call back;
- being outside with Dave, a fire, and the night sounds;
- playing tour guide for our friends and family;
- trying to get lost on day drives and finding new places;
- hiking in rhododendron tunnels and hopping rocks over river crossings;

- . . . and especially when I'm in my very own little cabin in the woods that Dave built on our land for me in 2020.

Masse Mountain has become our life brand. Masse Mountain isn't just a place. It's a state of mind and a set of guiding principles created and continuously shaped by our tiny stories. It's a custom filter that aids us in our every decision.

From this move, I've become a mother I actually like. I went from a yelling, short-fused mom and wife to the most chill AF mom you can imagine. The kids and Dave will *mostly* agree.

I wake up every morning and rarely think, *What do I have to do today?* Instead, I effortlessly greet my days with *What do I get to do today?* Seeking out a life that's so *right for you* (not settling and muddling through) feels more like a fun game you can't wait to show up for.

Instead of focusing on fixing Levi's behavioral problems, I turned to our living stories, read them, and let the insight lead us forward. The relationship he and I share now is deeply rooted in understanding.

Originally, I couldn't wait to send the kids to school, and that's what I did for a few years. Today, our kids are unschooled, which is a self-led, interest-based approach to education. When I saw who they were being conditioned to be, plus the outdated curriculum, that was enough for me. We pulled them out of the school system. We live like school doesn't exist . . . and we're thriving!

Currently, Kendall's into filmmaking, games, and experiencing richer friendships (because she has more time for them than a twenty-minute recess). Levi's verbally communicating his thoughts and emotions with more maturity than many grown men. Plus, how many other seven-year-olds do you know who are rocking a chain saw (often unsupervised at this point!) and axing fallen timber into firewood to sell?

All of the micro-changes we've made have been to craft a highly meaningful, storied life—one that feels custom-made only for us. The vibe in our home is far more warm and loving than before. I'm completely incubated in a lifestyle that kindles my continuous *becoming*.

What if *you* take what's hard in your life as an invitation for a wildly better life? What could that do for you? Your stories are exceptional guides, and they're accessible to you right now. Become a student of your stories, and learn how to read them as more than memories. Find your stories in your every emotion, observation, thought, intention, belief, goal, fear, wound, achievement, behavior, and action. Find them in every person, place, or thing in your life. Choose a word—*any word*!—and ask, What stories do I have around _____? Write a word or phrase for each tiny story that comes up.

If "it's not supposed to be this way" is calling you, too, be excited. Your stories will help you. Your stories have your back. Start by growing your list of stories, then look for the threads that link them together. Who knows what could happen? One thing's for sure: your life will shift in unexpected, cathartic ways. So slow down, take notice of your stories, and respond boldly . . . because one tiny story can change *everything*.

ABOUT THE AUTHOR

MARIE MASSE

Marie Masse (pronounced "moss") was a reliable rule follower. "You can do and be anything!" they said. The problem: she had no idea what she wanted. Mortgages were her life until one morning's traffic sparked the U-turn of a lifetime. Without a plan, she ditched the status quo to find aliveness.

Today, Marie sees adversity as an invitation to play. You'll find her savoring life on Masse Mountain, writing from her woodland cabin office made by her Canadian husband. Her daughter's creativity and her son's affinity for chain saws make for some meaningful days as an unschooling family. She's also a storytelling photographer and fierce advocate for neurodiversity.

She attributes her playful attitude and unwavering self-trust to her "story work." She founded Dangerously Good

Stories to help others find the hidden treasures in their stories because she believes . . .

One tiny story can change *everything*.

See the photo story from her
chapter: dangerouslygoodstories.com/elevate-photo-story

Chapter 9

LOVE THE SKIN YOU'RE IN

Stephanie Talia

"I learned to evaluate, reset, and keep going."

It felt like a bad dream.

I was awakened from a sound sleep by the alarm. It was like any other eighth-grade school day. I rolled over to shut the alarm off and remember feeling really sore and achy. Then an uncontrollable urge to scratch at my arms, legs, and body came over me. Still a little groggy, I caved in to the urge to scratch. Initially, it seemed like a good idea. Harmless, really, because it gave me relief.

Then five seconds later the overwhelming urge to scratch was back, and it just kept intensifying. I sat up in bed and looked at my skin. To my horror, my body was covered with red spots! They were all over my trunk, front and back. They were also on my upper thighs and arms, and a few were on my neck and face. I would say about 60 percent of my body was covered in red, angry, and inflamed skin. To make matters worse, the innocent scratching was not so innocent. I had scratched my skin so much that I was bleeding from ripping it open just to experience five seconds of relief. But I could not stop scratching.

I ran to the mirror. Shocked and horrified by what I saw, I felt tears welling up. I was in pain and completely confused. *What is this? What happened while I was sleeping that caused me to wake up like this?* When I'd gone to bed, my skin had been fine. I started to panic. I called for my mom. All of my thoughts, feelings, and anxiety were confirmed when she stepped into the room and looked at me. "Oh my God!" she said. "You're bleeding!" Tears came to her eyes. "Are you okay?" I don't recall what I said in response, but I do know I burst into tears. I just wanted to curl up in a ball and disappear. I was in pain, and I felt ugly and hopeless.

Needless to say, I did not go to school that day. We headed to the doctor to try to get to the bottom of this hellfire and get some relief quickly. The rest of the day was a blur. While in the doctor's office waiting to be seen, I tried to keep my mind occupied. I tried to ignore the overwhelming urge to scratch. So I made a game of it. I would sit on my hands and start counting: one, two, three, four, five . . . Twenty-five seconds was the longest I could last. My reward to myself was the lightest scratch— enough to satisfy the urge and not make my skin bleed more from scratching too hard or too much. Sometimes I was successful, sometimes I wasn't. The insatiable urge to scratch came from deep inside my skin and body, and it was relentless.

I'll never forget that day. I was young and hopeful that this would be like any other doctor visit: go in, explain the symptoms, get a prescription, take it, the problem goes away, done and move on. That is absolutely not how it went down. The doctor came in, and we explained what was going on. I was instructed to lift my shirt midway to expose my stomach, then turn around to show the same kind of red, angry, inflamed, painful spots on my back. I also lifted my sleeves to show that my arms matched my torso.

The doctor proceeded to tell my mom and me that I had psoriasis—Guttate psoriasis, to be exact. I was in the middle of a huge flare-up. My mom asked all the right questions. She wanted to know the who, what, when, where, and why, and how long it would take for it to go away. The doctor's response to "How long?" was "Forever; it is not curable." *I have psoriasis. I could have flare-ups for the rest of my life at any time.* Mom and I both left the doctor's office in tears. The doctor had given us a tube of 90+ percent tar-based cream that was to be applied on the affected areas until it went away.

That night I put the tar cream on my body everywhere I could reach, and my mom rubbed it everywhere I couldn't reach. It stank horribly. The smell lingered in my nose until I showered. The cream was thick and had a dirty coffee color, and it reeked. I cried every night for two weeks as I applied it on my body. I would go to bed hoping and praying that I would wake up the next day and the red scourge would be gone and I would no longer need the cream. The cream destroyed several of my white T-shirts. It stained them yellow, and they eventually had to be tossed, because no amount of bleach or washing would bring them back to crisp white. The tar cream did not heal my skin. It seemed to smother the psoriasis until it went away. To this day, I cannot drive through a road construction zone where they are putting blacktop down without memories of that tar cream flooding my mind. The smell of tar brings on an instant flashback and reminder of those evenings and that moment many, many years ago.

School brought a new kind of pain.

Going to school over the next several weeks was grueling, exhausting, and depressing. I hated school now that I had psoriasis. I tried to hide the inflamed red skin the best I could, but it would peek out of my clothing and give me away to my classmates. For two weeks I cried every morning in my room before I left the house for school. I had physical education every day, and I was itchy and sore, embarrassed, depressed, and self-conscious. I would not change in the locker rooms in front of the other girls so I could avoid questions and comments like, "What is wrong with you?" or "What is wrong with your skin?" or being told, "You have leprosy!" followed by pointing and laughing.

I would change in a bathroom stall, which was a chore in and of itself. I became quite skilled at undressing and getting dressed again without letting my clothes touch the toilet. Once dressed, I would take a deep breath, steel myself against any stares, and step out of the stall. I held my head high and acted like what I had just done was completely normal. There was nothing normal about it. I knew I was different. Hell, I *looked* different from all the other kids. My ugly, red, sore, and blotchy skin always gave me away. I could hide only so much of my psoriasis under my clothes. Inevitably someone always saw it or commented on it. After physical education, I would do the routine in the stall in reverse. I always felt better then, because I could cover up more of my skin. Getting fewer questions and stares and less pointing and laughing made it easier to get through the remainder of the day. The daily experience was exhausting. It made me feel small, ugly, hopeless, and lonely.

When I got home from school, I would go to my room, cry it out, and let it go. Then I would go downstairs and spend time with my mom, brothers, and dogs until my dad got home from work. We would then sit down together as a family for dinner.

I did not realize at the time just how much of a lifeline they all were for me. They helped me feel normal, accepted, loved, safe, and hopeful. I fit in there. I did not really fit in, nor was I fully accepted, at school, because I looked different. My family provided the stable and safe environment that helped me survive some tough times dealing with psoriasis and superficial friendships over the years. They were my strength when I wanted to give up and give in and felt completely hopeless. They led by example. It did not matter if people were different; they were all welcome in our house and at our table. I learned at an early age how to set boundaries, and that the only limits to my survival and to achieving my goals were those I put on them.

Life marches on.

Over the years I went through many cycles of psoriasis flare-ups. Some involved the dreaded tar cream, others required steroid cream to calm my skin. Every major life event that was over-the-top stressful, such as divorce, two cancer scares, and a career change brought new and unique psoriasis experiences and challenges.

I remember the day I had a major skin flare-up that was different from all the rest. It was everywhere, and different in how it looked and felt. The red, angry, and itchy skin was there, but the texture and appearance was completely different and ugly and horrible to look at. It was highly visible on my face, arms, and body. I had an inch-wide red, itchy area on my face. It stretched from ear to ear and up over my forehead, near my scalp line. My eyelids were swollen and sore and had dry, crusty patches on them. This was a first. My arms, legs, and torso had the usual hellfire with varying sizes of patchy red spots like my eyes all over. Again, the feeling of ugliness, embarrassment, hopelessness, and depression crept in and kept me from going out.

216

This was a particularly bad flare-up, and I was scheduled to interview for a new job in two weeks. I was in panic mode. No amount of makeup could hide what was so visible and ugly on my face. I could mostly hide what was on my body with clothes. The old insecure, depressing thoughts crept in. Now that I was older, I was concerned that I might not get the job because I looked different. I did not want to sit in a room of people, answering questions about my work accomplishments and successes over the years, and have them wonder what was wrong with me.

I quickly got in to see a dermatologist. The verdict: a psoriasis flare-up and an allergic reaction to fragrance. So many things made sense after seeing the dermatologist. I heeded her advice. I immediately stopped wearing makeup to allow my skin to chill and calm down. The problems weren't completely resolved by the time I went in for the interview, but I got creative and put on a lot of makeup that day. I recall thinking I looked like a clown. My eye shadow was heavier and darker than I normally wear it, but it helped me feel a little more confident and secure.

The interview experience was interesting and actually went quite well. I landed the job. I recently had a discussion with a senior leader who was part of the interview that day many years ago. I shared that I felt like I looked like a clown with all that makeup on because of my skin problems. She laughed and said no one had even noticed; rather, they were blown away by my confidence and professional accomplishments. It is funny how people's perceptions of situations can be so different.

It was a case of mind over matter. My drive to overcome obstacles and succeed in any situation comes directly from my mom and dad. They have always led by example. They taught my brothers and me that if we set goals, gave them our all, and worked toward them, we would be successful. Even if it was not pretty or a success on the first try, I learned to evaluate, reset, and keep going. If it matters and I want to achieve a goal . . . I never give up and I never quit! I also learned how to maintain a cool-as-a-cucumber facade. I may have been a jumbled mix of anxiety and nerves on the inside, but outwardly, I looked calm and in control. That enabled me to walk into many interviews with the mindset that I had already landed the job.

I keep learning.

My body has gotten very creative over the years in how psoriasis presents itself and where it decides to show up. Stress, staph, strep, upper respiratory infections, and fragrance allergies have all been contributing factors to my skin flare-ups throughout my lifetime.

Sometime around 2005 or so, the light bulb went on, and I had an aha moment. I'd been told and had just always thought that I had sensitive skin, because my skin would take exception to some products I used. I cannot even begin to quantify the amount of money and product that

I had thrown into the garbage over the years that had caused my skin to flare up or just hadn't worked. It all made sense now! At a very early age I could not use bubble bath, because it made my skin red, angry, itchy, and scaly.

I discovered that using steroid cream can thin the skin over time. I decided then that I did not want to depend on steroid or stinky creams for relief anymore. I wanted to have control, address the problems, and calm them naturally without having to run to the doctor or use some repulsive cream.

My quest for natural, transformational solutions began and has never stopped. I started researching and looking for natural solutions that would help and not harm my skin and body. I learned to read my product labels like I did the nutrition labels on food. With each new product I tried that worked, I became more hopeful, more confident. My mindset became more positive, and my skin tone and coloring began improving, too.

I have learned how to identify and deal with stress in situations to mitigate flare-ups. My body is my barometer. Ignoring things happening around me and in my environment is not an option.

Here are some important lessons I've learned:

- Have difficult conversations with people to talk things out instead of trying to ignore a problem.

- Walk away from toxic people or situations to evaluate whether it is important.
- Stop taking on other people's issues—the burden is theirs to own, not for me to shoulder.
- Use a lot of humor to defuse or lighten situations not only in the moment but also for myself. Laughing and humor are some of the best coping skills I use. They've kept me grounded in many difficult situations and enabled me to get through them and not only survive but thrive.

I choose my reality.

I have psoriasis; it's an autoimmune disease. It's something I deal with every single day.

I had a love/hate relationship with my skin from my midteens to my early thirties. Over the years, I've learned how to keep my emotions and stress in check. I have also learned how to keep my immune system strong so that my skin stays calm, which is the final piece of the puzzle.

Today, I control my psoriasis; it no longer controls me.

I am thriving, and I love the skin I am in.

Having someone tell me I have great skin is the best compliment I can receive. Several people have said that they did not even know I had skin issues until I told them. I have also been told that I look younger than my age. The first time I received a compliment like this, it made me tear up.

Compliments about my skin reinforce the importance of my purpose, journey, and mission, which is to share and offer hope to others and not to stay silent. I help educate and advocate for people who suffer because of skin problems. I love to share with others what I have learned over the years through my own journey and search for relief.

I give people H.O.P.E.

I **H**elp **O**pen **P**eople's **E**yes to natural, transformational solutions that I have personally vetted that help with inflammation of the skin and body. (Structured water, mud, minerals, salts, and botanicals are my go-to's to keep my skin and body issues in check.)

Even on my worst days, living through skin and body flare-ups, sitting on my hands, bleeding from ripping my skin open, hiding from people as well as receiving unwanted and unsolicited comments and questions, I found there is hope.

Don't give up, don't give in, and never quit!

I see you. I know your pain. I am you. There is hope.

ABOUT THE AUTHOR

STEPHANIE TALIA

Stephanie Talia learned at an early age what it was like to be different and to rise above it all to become successful in her career and business. She has been on a quest to love the skin she is in, figuratively and literally. Suffering from skin problems, and desperate for relief, she began her search for natural options and was relentless in the vetting of products.

After a long battle, she feels confident and beautiful in her skin. She educates and advocates for people who suffer because of skin problems. She gives people H.O.P.E.—she Helps Open People's Eyes to transformational solutions that not only solve skin issues but address the body as a whole, helping them truly live their best lives.

Learn more about Stephanie at www.stephaniesmindfulsolutions.com

Chapter 10

FIND PURPOSE IN THE UNEXPECTED

Dr. Brittany Clayborne

"Instead of measuring everything as it came to me, I practiced receiving it with grace."

"The phrase is *elephant in the room*!" I said to my mom as we sat in the living room watching *Wheel of Fortune*. My three-year-old son, Micah, was playing with Legos on the floor, and I was sitting in my rolling computer chair.

I leaned forward so that he could show me his newest creation. As I leaned back into my chair, I felt an eerie sensation. . . In the next three seconds I managed to yell, "Mom! Get Micah. I'm going to d—!" The pain arrested my words as it shot up my arm and into my jawbone, and then landed a final blow to my chest.

I could hear the ambulance sirens and the paramedic saying my name over his radio to the hospital staff as the incoming patient. I faded in and out of consciousness as I caught glimpses of the familiar skyline of our city whizzing by through the small, narrow window of the ambulance. Was I dreaming? I was twenty-nine, married with one child, and had a great job . . . just like I'd planned it.

I wasn't supposed to be in this ambulance. I wasn't supposed to be dying.

I heard voices . . .

"No! We can't touch her."

"Brittany, stay with us!"

"God, don't take my child!"

"Mommy is sleeping."

Warmth washed over me as I fought to hear the fading voices.

I tried to open my eyes, but the warmth wrapped around me like fresh sheets. . . . *Don't fight, just rest.* As I pulled the warmth in around me, I could hear a machine-like whirring in my ear. Then lightning struck my chest like a blow from Thor's hammer. The warmth was gone, and I was in immense pain all over. As I drew my first breath after death, I looked around—no longer afraid of dying but afraid of not *living.*

Plot twist. We've all heard the term. To put it lightly, it's a radical shift in the assumed outcome of a story.

I hadn't left any room in my story for a plot twist!

We don't leave room for a global pandemic, or for the loss of a job, a loved one, or a dream. Why should we? Those things seem increasingly unlikely, especially as we get farther into the plan. And because we have no flexibility in our plan, our plot twists can sometimes feel like major blows.

A plot twist can make it feel as if everything is rapidly burning before our eyes and we are standing helplessly and watching all the things we've worked for go up in smoke.

This is why they can be so dangerous. We don't expect them to affect things they are not akin to. I did not expect my heart failure to derail my corporate climb within a major airline, pummel my self-esteem, or affect my marriage, and yet it did all of those things in major ways. I watched myself seemingly "fall behind" my peers in life, love, and achievement, and I fell into a deep and lingering depression.

My plot twist had started long before that moment in the ambulance. It started on September 12, 2010, at 2:34 p.m., when I became a mother to my beautiful boy and a heart patient with a diagnosis of pregnancy-induced heart failure. The promise was that it would require just a pill or two per day for a few years to get my heart back to its healthy state . . . nothing else to manage the condition. Yet over the next seven years "just a pill or two" turned into several heart attacks. I thought I had hit rock bottom with my heart failure, but as time marched on, I was told I needed a mechanical heart to survive day-to-day activities like showering and making dinner. The mechanical heart meant I would soon need an actual heart transplant. I lived with my mechanical heart for two years and was finally lucky enough to receive a donor heart. I was counting on the promise of medical science that once I received my transplant, everything would get better. Yet during my ten-month post-transplant checkup I was told that stage 4 cancer had been found in my liver and in my spleen. The cancer presented as tiny specks, about three hundred of them in all. As if the chemo and radiation weren't bad enough, I was then plunged into the horror of divorce.

All within twenty-four months.

My story was no longer recognizable, not even by me.

On the days I felt well enough to rebuild from the ashes of my plot twist, I attempted to get my story back on track and pick up where I had left off. But I was no longer the twenty-nine-year-old with a three-year-old son and perfect marriage. I was now the thirty-four-year-old mechanical heart recipient, heart transplant survivor, and stage 4 cancer divorcee. So no matter how hard I tried to get back on the path I had planned, the winds of my plot twist continued to reroute my journey to a place where I had not prepared myself to exist.

Sitting there in the middle of my molten ash and the remnants of what had been my life, I realized that although the plot twist had destroyed a lot, it had not destroyed me. My health was gone. My marriage was gone. My career was gone. But I stood. I remained.

The "I" that remained was not one with career status, familial roles, or societal approval. The "I" that remained was the infrastructure of my soul. A beautiful openness prepared to be filled with passionate, intentional, and captivating moments that I was responsible for creating. In that realization I came to understand that the problem was not the plot twist.

The problem was *my perception* of the plot twist.

I had given the circumstances power over my entire being, and in doing so I had inadvertently authorized my ego to lead my life in a mindless charge of self-pity, bitterness, and lack of self-love.

So I decided that *I should be the plot twist*. It's my story! Why shouldn't I be the radical shift?

Think about some of the greatest stories of our time:
- What if Rapunzel had let her gal pals climb up her hair, and declared sisters before misters?
- What if the Big Bad Wolf had had asthma?
- What if the Three Bears had had a blow-up mattress and made a little extra porridge?
- What if Cinderella had set an alarm?

The outcome of each of those timeless tales would have been radically different. So I fired my ego and promoted my soul, not in an effort to rebuild my old life, but with a plan to create a new, beautiful, and soul-satisfying reality that I would be proud to own, live, and declare as mine.

The first thing I needed to do was release the manifold facades that my ego had created over the previous ten years and dig to the foundation of my soul to find my true self. I had become so tied up in fulfilling my roles as a wife, mother, worker, and, most recently, as a patient that I hadn't even realized that those roles had become who I thought I was. I was stuck in a cycle that I had created for myself because I had become obsessed with weighing my worth by my roles.

So when my son was disappointed, I felt worthless as a mother.

When my husband signed the divorce papers, I felt worthless as a wife.

When I couldn't return to work because of my health, I felt worthless as an employee.

This was my first aha moment. It wasn't about my health or my relationship with others, it was about my relationship with myself and my failure to identify myself as innately valuable. So I had to ask myself some questions:

If my worth is tied to these roles, who am I without them?

Who was I before them?

Did they give me value, or were they given to me because I am valuable?

Do you see what I was doing here? I was so programmed to think that my identity was validated by my roles that even in these questions I was still trying to attach my worth to something or someone. So I needed to get comfortable with the idea that *I am innately worth it.*

I needed to help myself remember that I am worth it without condition, so I went to the root of it all. The last time I had felt worth it without condition was when I was told that a heart donor had been found for me.

On that day, I was alone at the hospital. I had just ordered dinner and was frustrated that I couldn't be at home with my family or even at work (another realization that my worth was tied to my doing and being). My doctor called and said, "Brittany, we have a heart for you." I remember being overwhelmed with relief, fear, grief, wonder, and many other things. The depth of selflessness and love for humanity that is required to allow another person to live when one cannot is paramount, and in that moment, I remember feeling valuable. I didn't feel the need to question if I deserved it or if someone else had done more to earn it. And because the donor's life was over, I couldn't do anything to reciprocate or make myself valuable enough to receive it. So there I sat, arrested by gratefulness.

Gratefulness. That was the key to understanding my unmerited worth.

Instead of measuring everything as it came to me, I was just going to practice receiving it with grace. I was going to receive it. I was going to be open to the thought that I am inherently worthy and deserve good things.

Once I allowed myself to receive with gratefulness, amazing things began to happen in my life. I was given many opportunities to grow, change, and step into new understandings of myself, my world, and the conditions around me, all because I was receiving. Not only receiving but receiving with grace and not with guilt.

Then one day I was answering some interview questions via email for a magazine article. One thing I like to do when proofreading my own work is to try reading it as though I'm seeing it for the first time. As I read, I realized how hard I was on myself! I wasn't giving myself any credit for surviving. I credited my family for caring for me. I credited friends for praying with me and being a listening ear. I credited my medical team for their various roles, but not once did I acknowledge my own strength, tenacity, or fortitude in the midst of my multiple health scares. I knew that I was valuable. I knew that it was okay to receive. But I had to learn to receive from my biggest critic of all.

Myself.

So I sat at my desk and began to write:

Dear Brittany,

I looked at you today, and I saw that you are beautiful. I knew that, but it gets lost sometimes. There are so many other things that are pulling me, pulling my focus away, and I never really just look at you. I listened to you today too. The words that you used, the confidence with which you speak, the way that you say I love you, the way you speak to Micah when you realize the miracle that he is. I watched you work. You truly love what you do. You want so badly to use the things that you have learned on your journey to help others with theirs. That passion and tenacity is so incredible, it's like a light that shines from within you when you are sure that you're exactly where you want to be.

I need you to remember how much you wanted to live when you were dying, and live that life now.

Know that I love you. Know that I am proud of you for so many things, and for so many reasons, and in so many ways.

All of my endless love,

Me

That is what I needed. I needed to see myself from another point of view, and that was it. On that day I saw my soul. I saw the deepest and most beautiful parts of myself and allowed her to be loved, to be seen, to be heard, and to be vulnerable.

When we see vulnerable things, we embrace them. We champion them. We cheer and fight for them harder because we know that their survival is fragile.

Behind all the calloused and broken pieces of ourselves, our stories, our what-ifs and could-have-beens, we find the fragility of our souls, and that is the part of ourselves that we must be brave enough to discover, embrace, and carry into our new story.

My plot twist was my health, and I couldn't be more grateful for the lessons that it has taught me. I know so much more about myself than I ever would have learned if everything had gone according to plan.

Here are a few other things that I was taught by becoming my own plot twist and reclaiming my story:

- Faith in something is good. Faith in *yourself* is vital.
- Being "stuck" has nothing to do with being physically unable to move; rather, it has to do with the inability to evolve mentally, physically, and spiritually.
- Unconditional love of others requires unconditional love of self.

- Finding purpose and peace is more important than anything the world has to offer.
- Purpose is more important than the plan.

Knowing who I truly am now, knowing my purpose, passion, and what I am truly meant to bring into the world, I realize that the plan I made would never have satisfied me. My plan would not have quenched the fire that I felt burning within myself to be more. My plan may have pacified me for a while. It may even have given me years of memories and great moments, but it wouldn't have given me the most important thing that I have received.

Love for myself and understanding of my innate worth.

Today I hold a doctor of psychology degree and am solely focused on helping other people find their beautiful fragility, teaching them how to love it, and watching them become the plot twist in their own stories.

ABOUT THE AUTHOR

DR. BRITTANY CLAYBORNE

At age 26, Brittany Clayborne found herself propelled into her destiny after unexpected heart failure and a diagnosis of stage 4 cancer. Finding little to no support for the mental health of critically ill patients, Brittany earned her Doctorate in Psychology in order to help others navigate the type of journey that she had faced.

Primarily engaging audiences as a speaker, Dr. Brittany offers a personal and vulnerable look at the human experience. She shares her journey providing equal parts insight, humor, and the intent to help others.

Born and raised in New Orleans, Dr. Brittany draws the city's deep love of music as a classically trained percussionist. She shares this love of music with her son, Micah. When they aren't having a jam session they enjoy traveling, watching New Orleans Saints football, and swimming. Both also share a passion for helping adults and children improve mental health through their nonprofits, Brittany Speaks and Micah Gives, respectively.

To catch up with Dr. Brittany on the daily, follow @drbrittanyspeaks on Facebook, Instagram, & TikTok or visit brittanyspeaks.com

Chapter 11

DISCOVER ANSWERS IN THE UNKNOWN

Kofi Williams

"I didn't get the clarity and the answer I needed when I expected it, but it came, as I knew it would."

I needed a mental health break, and not just a typical day or two of hibernation. I desperately needed a break from everyone and everything. After a year of pandemic isolation, social injustice, traumatic media reports, and collective trauma, I just wanted to numb out. I sat staring at my computer screen, my heart seeming to pound outside of my body. With a deep inhale, I secretly hit the Book Flight button on a one-way ticket out of the country.

It was July 2021. I was a vibrant, active, fly sixty-one-year-old with plenty more life to live. I was the CEO of me, setting my own hours, working within the comfortable surroundings of my beautiful apartment, doing work I loved, helping women create and live the highest vision for their life. Yet I felt drained, fatigued, and depleted, with little left to give.

I'd spent the previous ten years empowering women and growing a thriving coaching business. In 2016, I walked away from a thirty-year administrative career and within two years doubled my salary. I was living the life I'd dreamed of: long morning walks, afternoon naps, and helping women live the life they'd postponed. But I had this restless, inner calling to do much more and impact the lives of even more women. But how could I when I had nothing left to give? The question for me then became, how do I want to show up for the next ten years?

Ten Years in the Making

I looked at the registration numbers. . . . *Four*! One was my sister, who later texted that she hadn't noticed the date when she registered and wouldn't be able to attend my ten-year anniversary masterclass. The other was a girlfriend who I'm certain was simply trying to be supportive. And although I appreciated the other two registrants, I wanted to touch many more lives.

My chest slowly deflated as I let out a deep exhale. That's how my spirit felt too—deflated. The day wasn't only my ten-year coaching anniversary, but also my sister Teresa's birthday. She would have turned fifty-four. I'd lost her ten years earlier to that bitch cancer, and she is my Why. Helping women live free, full, and abundant lives is my life purpose. I'm crystal clear on both.

Over the previous ten years, I'd helped hundreds of women break through their limitations and do more than they thought they could. And although I desperately wanted to help even more women, I found myself in need of help. I was reminded of an Instagram post that read, "You deserve to be filled the same way you pour." And at that time in my life, I desperately needed filling.

Each year I do something special to commemorate Teresa's July 14 birthday. I intentionally took my coaching certification exam on that day. I got my first tattoo on that day; of course, it was her name. I've gotten several body piercings over the years on that special day. I've taken dream trips. Made life-changing decisions and, most recently, shaved my fourteen-year-old, waist-length locks. It has become a day symbolic of liberating action and life transition for me and a love gift to her. But this year . . . in my current mental and emotional state, I couldn't find the motivation to do much.

Unwilling to break the tradition of honoring my sister and it being my ten-year coaching anniversary, I had promised my audience a big announcement, when in reality I had nothing . . . until I got a message from a little redbird.

Teresa's birthday fell on a Wednesday—"Go Live Day" in the LIGHTbeamers Facebook Community, led by my good friend April Pertuis. It's a community where I learn and practice storytelling and broadcasting skills. I've had the honor of being a featured speaker at two of the LIGHTbeamers Live Storytelling Symposiums.

Each Wednesday, we're provided a prompt and challenged to come as we are, hit the big red button, go live, and practice in a safe, supportive community. Broadcasts are unscheduled and can be done anywhere within Wednesday's twenty-four-hour window, which means you could have one live viewer to several—or none at all. Other community members watch the replay and provide supportive comments. It's all voluntary, loving, inclusive, and safe.

I had not done a live broadcast in a while. Sitting on my couch feeling sorry for myself, I figured the least I could do was show up live on Teresa's birthday, right? The day's prompt was "What Are Some of Your Healthy Habits?" When I logged on to go live, I was greeted by a beautiful ray of light just beginning her broadcast. I decided to support her before I went live. It was just the two of us.

Her name was Sheri. I knew the name, because we were both LIGHTbeamer OGs (Original Girls), having been members since the community's birth five years earlier. But I couldn't recall ever seeing one of her broadcasts. I'm certain I would have remembered, because I was automatically drawn to her light. She was broadcasting outdoors, under a towering, mature tree, its vibrant, huge green leaves her backdrop. The setting sun provided natural highlights as it peeked through her flowing brown hair. The entire scene looked ethereal as she spoke.

"Today, I'm making history by being one of the OGs in the LIGHTbeamers Community who has *never* gone live! When I saw today's prompt, I had this strong feeling that I was supposed to go live. But that's like pure torture for me! Why would I be told to do that? I said, 'God if I'm supposed to do a live today, I want you to send me some redbirds.'"

She went on to share that God had told her ten years earlier that he'd show her many things through redbird revelations, and that it has proved true countless times throughout the years.

But she was at a hotel in the concrete jungles of Dallas, a two-hour drive from her home. Where was she going to find a redbird? She had been there three days already. She'd seen birds, but not a red one.

She looked and looked for redbirds that day—for her sign. They didn't show up, but that nagging feeling that she was supposed to go live did. She had lunch with her husband . . . but still no redbird. So, she asked again, attempting to quiet that inescapable, nagging "go live" voice.

"'God, I *really* don't want to do this broadcast! So, if I'm supposed to, please send me a redbird so it's sure confirmation that I'm supposed to do this today.'"

As she walked back to her hotel, a bird flew by. . . .

It was a female redbird! That Sheri really knows her redbirds; she explained that the females are lighter in color than the males.

Now wait a minute, she said to herself. *Was that really a redbird?* Her debilitating fear of going live made her desperately hope she'd been wrong. When she turned in the direction the bird flew, she saw to her surprise not one redbird—but two! A brighter-colored male had joined the female. I can imagine God smiling and doing a "mic drop!"

Sheri said, "I guess I'm going to have to do this live today," although she was still uncertain why and resisted with every fiber of her being. But she had asked for a sign and received it. Now she had to be obedient and act on it.

How many times have you been given signs and ignored them out of fear? What do you think would be different about your life if you acted on them?

Now, I don't know why I chose to listen to that broadcast at that exact time on that day. I often feel guilty about not having the time to watch and support more of the community members' broadcasts. I usually just record mine and go back to my busy life. But today, at this appointed time, I was inexplicably drawn to this woman. She even posted photos of the redbirds and shared them in the comments later. This was for real!

I sat there on my couch, tears streaming uncontrollably down my face as I typed the following in her comments:

> Wow! Your story was amazing. I hope you continue doing lives. Ironically, today is my sister's birthday. She would have been 54. She transitioned 10 years ago. Every time I see a redbird, I feel it's her. When she first passed, I lived in a house and this little redbird would come sit on the windowsill. Hearing your story of not one but two redbirds on her birthday was very powerful and inspiring for me. It was as if she sent you and your message to encourage me to keep doing the work I was placed here to do. Thank you!

Sheri replied with this note:

> God bumps! I promise you it was for you. I do not love speaking on camera, but I knew I had to today. That's the Lord's loving kindness. Happy heavenly birthday to your sister. I know you miss her terribly, but oh the celebration she's having. Glory!!! Love you, Kofi. You are a gem!

This beautiful unfolding story is the power of being in community with like-minded people.

It's the story of learning to listen to your soul.

It's the story of being brave enough to face your fears.

It's the story of learning new skills and tools and knowledge to create the life that you want.

It's a testimony to how stretching and growing create a bigger life experience.

It's about being obedient to that still, small voice, even if you're afraid and even if you don't know how.

I'd been teaching and modeling these life-transforming lessons to women for the past ten years and desperately wanted to share them with even more women. But how?

God was like, "Okay, I see you need a little more proof. Hold tight. . . ."

The redbirds lifted my spirits. But still, it was July 14, my sister's birthday, and I had nothing to give—and what I did have to offer felt halfhearted and not right with my spirit. I was scheduled to go live in an hour for a masterclass. I had envisioned my biggest audience showing up on this day. It was going to be that special thing I do each year to commemorate Teresa. It turned out my entire audience was going to be maybe two people. My heart just wasn't in it. I pushed the Cancel button.

A half hour later, my phone dinged with this message: "Your funds are on the way!" I hadn't signed any new coaching clients, so I figured it must be a duplicate or a mistake.

Logging on to my payment account, I discovered someone had purchased a coaching package!

I have each new client complete an intake form. The last question asks, "What else would you like me to know about you?" What my new client wrote floored me!

> I heard you at a women's conference in Dallas—
> the one where the oldest female bodybuilder
> was appearing. You spoke, and I have been
> following you on and off since. Your words were
> very instrumental in my life at a very critical time. I
> believe I'm at another critical time. ~Vanessa

That conference had been more than five years earlier. I'd had the honor of sharing the stage with Ernestine Shepherd, the "world's oldest female bodybuilder," at a women's conference in Dallas. She was eighty years young at the time. She's eighty-six as I write this, and still going strong! More proof that it's never too late to live a life of personal freedom, whatever that looks like for you—you get to decide.

My heart was so happy! Not because I sold a coaching package, but because this was another reminder that I had unknowingly made a difference in someone's life! This is the feeling that I love, and women like Vanessa, who are active participants in their own liberation, are the women I enjoy working with most.

And as if the redbirds and this confirmation weren't enough . . . I was tagged in this Facebook post on that same day, still my sister's birthday:

> Today marks three years that I began my coaching journey in Dallas under co-trainer Kofi Williams. What an incredible three years it has been. I will never forget Kofi telling us that we had to get through our own crap before we could help anyone else. I took this to heart and have worked tirelessly on letting go of the things that don't serve me, grabbing ahold of adventure, risk, and abundance in a way that I never allowed myself before.
>
> Three years later I can say I am truly on the path to becoming the best version of myself. My coaching business is flourishing and offers me the flexibility and freedom to serve my clients and make a great living from anywhere. I no longer worry about a work life balance; I just live a balanced life. ~Katie

By now, I was feeling what Sheri must have felt, seeing the redbirds. I said, "Okay, God, I get it!" I have made a difference. I am making a difference. And I've always known in my heart that I was placed here to make an even greater difference in the lives of women.

But I still have no idea how I'm going to go from helping hundreds to helping thousands. Maybe I'll find my answers during my travels, one of those Eat-Pray-Love-type of experiences, you know? Maybe that's why God's sending me on this international journey. I just know that I'm supposed to go. And just like Sheri, I'm being obedient to that still, small voice.

In the meantime, Teresa's birthday came and went . . . and I still had no clue how I was supposed to serve more women. I was determined not to proclaim, post, or email my audience until I had clarity on how I was supposed to move forward with this next chapter of my coaching business and my life. I knew I wanted to do work that felt good to my soul. I loved what I did, but sometimes I felt drained giving so much of myself.

The next morning, July 15, Sheri posted this message on my Facebook wall. . . . "Look closely, Kofi. This one is for you today." Attached was a photo of a single redbird in a green field! I knew it was Teresa saying, "Don't give up, sis. I'm right here with you, and remember, you promised to tell my story."

I asked Sheri, just to be certain, "Was this actually taken today or is it something you had on your phone already?"

She replied, "This is for real, today, and it's for you!"

Two days after Teresa's birthday and my ten-year anniversary as a coach, I still had no message about how I was to live my next chapter. One thing I knew for certain:

my sensitive spirit was tired, and I would no longer water people who didn't want to grow.

I had the luxury of a full day to myself. But worrying about making my "big anniversary announcement" was taking up a lot of my energy. As a certified energy practitioner, I knew the power of releasing negative energy, so I chose to do so. You can learn more about my ninety-minute energy intensive at www.coachkofi.com/assessment.

I decided I would simply email my tribe and post my honest truth.

> I haven't figured out what I want this next chapter of my life to look like . . . *yet*! I've purchased a one-way ticket out of the country. I'll be back next year. Between now and then, I know I'll figure it out. Come join me on this journey through my blog. ~Love, Coach Kofi

But before I sent the email and made the post, I decided to enter my think tank—a long hot shower. I did what I have my clients do: I asked a better question.

Rather than *how*, I asked, *Kofi, who do you want to work with?*

Women like me, I said.

Okay, describe women like you.

- strong desire to live a fuller, richer life
- mature
- single by choice or circumstance
- independent
- high achieving
- limited circle of like-minded friends
- desire to live a life of personal freedom
- open to healthy dating, even marriage, but okay if it doesn't happen
- conscious
- lonely
- active
- lifelong learners or open to learning
- may be a Nana, a Gigi, a Mimi, or a Gran Gran, but still fly and sensuous

Then I asked myself, *Okay, great! How do you enjoy helping women, Kofi?*

- speaking
- writing
- teaching
- inspiring
- motivating
- coaching
- living the example

By the time I got out of the shower, I had the clarity, direction, message, and ideal audience for this next chapter of my life along with a work/life balance that felt good to my soul! That night in the shower, a new movement was birthed, a community for women ready to master the art of being authentically themselves and fearlessly living it.

We've raised the kids, been dedicated employees, wives, and girlfriends, even side chicks, tried marriage and love—more than once. We still love the thought of love, but we're just fine if it doesn't happen again. We no longer need to settle. We are no longer waiting on friends or family. We've sacrificed, usually at our own expense, but now find ourselves alone, lonely, and rediscovering who we are, or maybe discovering ourselves for the first time.

It's our time to do all the things we've promised ourselves we would do once (insert your promise here . . . the kids were grown, we retired, found the right man, hit XX age, paid off some bills, went back to school, lost XX number of pounds . . . You know the list, right?).

What are your unkept promises?
Do you dream of travel or living abroad—as I'm doing?
Do you daydream of relocating?
Planting a garden?
Writing a book?
Starting a business?
Taking a sabbatical?
Attending wellness retreats?
Lounging on a beach reading?
Starting a hobby?
Doing passion work?

Spend some quiet time with these questions: *What are my unkept promises to myself? What is holding me back? How do I want to live? How do I want to feel?*

I didn't get the clarity and the answer I needed when I expected it, but it came, as I knew it would. Delayed does not mean denied. I didn't know how. But all the while, I was doing the work I teach in my courses: embracing silence, meditating, affirming how I want to feel, visualizing the people I want to help and the life I will live, gaining new knowledge, connecting with like-minded women who are where I'm striving to go, shifting negative energy, being mindful, believing in my purpose even when I don't know how to make it happen, and loving myself in spite of. That's how you create a life you love to live, and I want to empower every woman to do so.

I teach everyone in my community two key principles:

1. The work always works when you work the work.
2. The first relationship to work on is the one with yourself.

It looks like I did do something significant after all for Teresa's birthday. I launched a movement!

ABOUT THE AUTHOR
KOFI WILLIAMS

Kofi Williams was an inner-city teen mom battling clinical depression, anxiety, and low self-esteem for the first half of her life. She was also intelligent, intuitive, and driven.

At a traumatic crossroads—turning fifty, losing her youngest sister, and going through a fourth divorce—she was introduced to ten powerful words: "When you change your thinking, you can change your life."

This began a never-ending love affair of personal development, self-discovery, and healing. Along the way, Kofi discovered herself and her purpose: to help women heal and live the highest version of themselves.

A holistic lifestyle coach, speaker, and author, Kofi lives what she teaches. She travels from country to country as a digital nomad, coaching, leading retreats, and empowering women to "live more life and be more you."

To learn more about Kofi's online community, self-guided courses, coaching programs, and retreats, visit www.kofiwilliams.com

If you are ready to learn how to live more life and be more you, you're invited to join www.kofiwilliams.com/community

Chapter 12

RECOGNIZE YOUR GIFTS

Tessa Kidd

"What makes you
uniquely you can be
used to muster joy
and serve others."

"Just a mom."

I envisioned those three little words emblazoned on my tombstone. I was going to be the Big 4-0. Holy crap. What is it about turning forty that makes us reassess our life choices?

Shouldn't I have accomplished more in my life by now? Is this it for me? I wondered.

I'd had a beautiful life and had zero regrets, yet there I was, facing my fortieth turn around the sun, and thinking, *If my time were to end tomorrow, what would my legacy be? What would be said of me at my funeral?*

I'd never gotten around to finishing that degree or completing that book I'd been secretly working on for a while. Who had the time or energy? I'd spent years following my husband from move to move, supporting him and living wherever the navy positioned him. Chris would always repeat an old joke that his dad, also a career navy seaman, used to say to his mom whenever she complained about having to uproot their lives yet again: "If the navy had wanted us to have a wife, they would have issued us one." Meaning, we married into this life, so we had to accept that this was the way it was going to go. And I believe my mother-in-law and I both did, to the very best of our abilities.

Chris and I wanted to have a family, so between deployments and cross-country moves, and after suffering the devastating miscarriage of our daughter, we went on to have three babies back-to-back. It's just how it worked out for us. I wouldn't change a thing, and I would do it all over again, even knowing the great loss we would have to endure.

"I really don't want a party, babe. I want something different, something more meaningful."

My sweet husband was trying to coax me out of the funk I'd been in for weeks. I was positive I did not want a party, and I knew for sure I wanted to mark this milestone birthday differently, but how or doing what, I had no clue.

He knew how much I loved party planning, and it was a well-played move to offer up the idea of hosting a huge family gathering to get me to perk up. He knew our closest friends and family would definitely make the six-hour drive. And those friends who could get to us only by plane would undoubtedly make the trip to join us. We had moved to South Carolina from our home state of Florida just a few months earlier, and I was dealing with some serious homesickness. Unlike previous moves, this one felt permanent. We were no longer on temporary orders from the navy to relocate and make our home on another base for a few short years. Rather, we were moving voluntarily, in pursuit of a new job that would provide financial stability for our family and more opportunities for Chris to grow in his engineering career. We were setting down roots two states away. Never mind the fact that we would be leaving our home and everyone we loved. We had to go where the job search led us.

On top of missing my family and friends, I'd spent my recent days thinking about how quickly the years had gone by. Our children were ten, nine, and eight years old. I just couldn't shake the guilt I felt that I was not where I thought I should be in life. It's a dreadful feeling to look around and know in your heart that you are blessed beyond measure yet still feel like you are somehow failing at life.

What was missing? Chris had a great job, we lived in a nice house, and our kids were healthy, thriving, and doing well in school. As for me . . . I was doing just what I—we—had planned for me to do. I had given up any shot at a career and was living that mom life. I was Mom'ing, and I was darn good at it. Why was that not enough?

Around this time, a Facebook campaign promoting a ministry to sponsor children in Rwanda crossed my feed. Their plea was simple: thirty-nine dollars a month afforded a young boy or girl the chance to attend school, receive a proper education, and be provided hot meals. We decided to sponsor a girl. As sponsors, we also had the ability to send more food supplies, clothing, hygiene necessities, mattresses, bedsheets, and mosquito nets. We could even purchase a goat or two to provide the families with fresh milk—all in an effort to offer hope and help improve their quality of life.

After about a month or so, I checked in on my feelings. Was this meaningful enough? We had chosen Gasel intentionally because we estimated she was the same age our daughter would have been, had she lived. We wanted to honor our girl's life by supporting another girl, yet I still felt I could be doing more.

"She's one of the lucky ones," we were told. Her mother, father, and siblings had survived the 1994 Rwandan genocide and were living with her. She was the oldest of five children. They were poor, but they had a home and each other, and that was more than I could say for a lot of the other children.

Soon after we started sponsoring our girl, we read about an orphan boy who was in desperate need of a sponsor. Bahati was his name. His story moved us to tears. He was the only member of his family to survive the genocide. For years he had lived on the streets, and he would often hang around the church, where he could be heard enjoying the music and singing. He was also a gifted musician. One time, when he was allowed to give the drums a go, the volunteers marveled at how he was naturally gifted rhythmically and vocally. He exuded joy from every ounce of his being anytime he was allowed to express himself through music or song. A church volunteer took pity on him and had taken him in, in hopes of finding him a sponsor. Because his needs were significant—he had no place to live, no family to speak of, and so on—whoever chose to sponsor him would need to commit more than just a monthly payment. Bahati needed a *family*.

Looking back, I know this was divinely orchestrated. It was his bright smile and haunting eyes I saw in the photo that was shared. The joy I could see in his smile contradicted the sadness in his eyes. My heart went out to him. After reading his story, Chris and I spent hours talking about him and what it would mean to take on the responsibility of sponsoring another child—especially one whose needs were greater than just the monthly financial commitment. I went to bed that night unable to think of anything else but Bahati. I woke up very early the next morning, and before anyone else stirred, I reached out to the woman who had shared his story:

"We would like to sponsor Bahati. What do we do next?"

"Come to Rwanda, Tessa! Meet your son."

I read those words on the screen, then blinked and read them again a few more times.

Rwanda? Africa? What?

The thought had never occurred to me, but as soon as I read her words, the idea quickly took root deep in my heart, and suddenly, I found what I was searching for: purpose.

My response was two words. "I'm coming."

Rwanda is nicknamed the Land of a Thousand Hills because it is surrounded by volcano mountain ranges and endless rolling hills. For a small, landlocked country, the scenery is absolutely breathtaking. Mountains, volcanos, rivers, crater lakes, terraced mountainsides, seemingly endless tea and sunflower fields, and montane forests are why people come to Rwanda to commune with nature. Rwandans have a saying: "God roams the world but comes to rest in Rwanda." Her beauty is unmatched. Even God knew He had done some of His best work when He created beautiful Rwanda. It's easy to understand why once one visits, one can never erase her from memory.

In the spring of 1994, I was twenty-one years old. If you're like me, you might vaguely remember something about Rwanda being mentioned on the world news stage, but that's all. My biggest worry was thinking about what I was going to do with the rest of my life. I had been attending community college off and on since graduating high school in 1990, but I had no real direction as to where I wanted to go with that. I didn't know exactly what I wanted to be when I grew up. That restlessness led me to complete a few vocational studies that eventually set me up for decent jobs in the medical and hotel and travel industries. I bounced from job to job, searching for my calling. I was good at each of those jobs, and every supervisor I had would encourage me and say, "You've got a bright future in such and such, if you really want it." But no matter what job I took, it didn't feel like I was fulfilling my purpose— whatever that was. Right around that time, I should have been looking forward to my college graduation or, at the very least, starting out on a career path.

My point is I was in my own bubble. I had no inkling about what was going on in my own country, let alone clear across the globe in Africa. I was self-absorbed and oblivious to the fact that over the course of a hundred days, Rwandans would endure such brutality that when all was said and done, 800,000 of them were left dead—many of them women, children, and the elderly. Entire generations of families gone, just like that. When I learned that fact, it wrecked me. I am extremely close to my family, and the thought that we could be living peacefully one day and then wiped out completely by evildoers the next was devastatingly heartbreaking to imagine. Rwanda was never on my radar, and it certainly was never on my places-to-visit bucket list. It just wasn't somewhere I ever thought of visiting.

Six months after that text conversation, I found myself on a plane headed to Africa with no clue whether anyone would actually be waiting for me once I landed. The meaningful fortieth birthday present I had asked for and that my loving husband had obliged was finally here. I made it to Rwanda safe and sound. We landed in the dark of night, and I couldn't help but notice the irony of it all. Here I was leaping into the literal unknown, and I literally could not see where I was landing. However, I believe it was that leap of complete and utter faith that led me to one of the most incredible and unforgettable experiences I have ever had. One that would change my world perspective and the course of my life forever. One that would change how I see myself as a mom and a human being.

Three weeks in Rwanda. Twenty-one days. That's all I had. When I made my way to the gate, there was my beautiful, smiling host, waiting and waving excitedly at me. A big sign that said *"Murakaza neza"* ("Welcome") hung on a wall. I felt a huge surge of relief. After flying 7,545 miles and a torturous twelve-hour delay in London because of mechanical problems, I wasn't alone anymore. I had made it. Jet lag forgotten and aches aside, I got my second wind and wanted to hit the ground running. My excitement at being in this beautiful, new country and meeting my son was palpable. I could not contain myself!

From the airport, I was whisked away to the guesthouse and allowed just enough time to drop off my baggage and freshen up. We needed to get on another bus for two more hours to make the trek to the village where my boy was waiting. The moment Bahati and I locked eyes for the first time, we were both overcome with emotion. We walked carefully toward each other until we were mere inches apart. Then we embraced as if our lives depended on it and both broke down in tears. It felt like hours before we let go and I said I wanted to get a good look at his face. He laughed. Such a mom thing to do and say, right? I felt an instant connection with him, and from that moment on, I truly saw him as my son.

I would go on to spend three precious weeks with Bahati, getting to know him, visiting his school, meeting some of his teachers and friends, and seeing where he lived. I met his house mom, Mama Jackie, who was assigned to care for Bahati and seventeen other young boys in a small, humble home on the school grounds. I was also given the opportunity to see more of the country, to be fully immersed in the culture, to practice my limited knowledge of their native language, Kinyarwanda, and to learn about the horrific atrocities of the 1994 Rwandan genocide.

I spent some of those days taking tours at memorial sites, listening to harrowing stories from other adult survivors, playing with groups of children, helping students practice English, and, my favorite part, participating in home visits. On home visits, our team would go to some of the newly sponsored students' homes to meet their families, get to know them a little, and offer them food and supplies. These visits were always eye opening and deeply moving, because the living situations varied greatly. Some families were extremely poor and had makeshift homes where multiple children and their parents or a guardian slept crammed together on the dirt floor, with virtually nothing else to call their own. Others had small but decent living spaces with designated bedrooms or a makeshift kitchen area. One thing remained the same: all the students and their families were delighted to welcome us into their homes no matter how they appeared. They took pride in sharing what little they had to make their guests feel comfortable.

When we visited Gasel, her mama saw our bus headed in their direction way before we arrived. We later learned that she was so excited to be welcoming visitors that she ran all the way home from wherever she was visiting, went to her neighbor's house, and borrowed their only chair and the husband's shirt just so she could wear something over her tattered housedress and offer a seat to one of us. Looking around her humble home, it was easy to see she did the best she could to add beauty to her surroundings. At one point, she disappeared, only to reappear with a plastic bag full of the letters, cards, and photos I had sent over the last year. She spoke no English, but she grabbed the stack and, while nodding and smiling, pressed my letters to her chest and repeatedly said the one phrase I didn't need a translator to understand: "Murakoze cyane" ("Thank you very much"). I felt her deep appreciation for my simple offerings.

Gasel was all smiles but very shy. She hid behind her mama most of the visit, only answering briefly the questions our translator asked for me. Things like *What's your favorite subject in school?* Math. *What do you want to be when you grow up?* A doctor or engineer. When our time came to an end and it was time to leave, Gasel and her mama hugged me hard. I left feeling like we had truly formed a connection in our brief time together.

That same day we made several home visits, and a group of us were walking toward the next village. I noticed a young mom carrying her naked baby on her hip, keeping up with our pace. I smiled at her, and she smiled back. The next thing I knew, she handed me her baby. Caught off guard, I did what any mom does naturally—I smiled at the surprised baby and bounced her in an effort to keep her from crying. I thought maybe her mama just wanted a break and for me to hold her for a bit. Imagine my surprise when her mama took off running. I looked over at our guide, and he immediately extended his arms, gesturing for me to give him the baby. When the baby was safely in his arms, he shook his head and took off in the direction her mama had gone. Later we would learn that sometimes, in an act of desperation, young moms would do that—hand their babies to American strangers, assuming that whatever life we could provide would be better than the one she had to offer and in hopes that we would take her baby home and raise him or her as one of our own. Can you imagine feeling so hopeless that you believe your baby is better with a stranger than she is with you, her own mother? Heartbreaking.

I had many little experiences during those few weeks that continued to open my eyes and break my heart wide open. The beautiful moments are forever etched on my heart, and the terrible parts I witnessed I can never "unsee," nor will I ever forget them. More importantly, I saw firsthand how this beautiful country had not only healed but flourished in the aftermath of the genocide. I realized that every child should be allowed to dream of a better future, and I learned about the healing power of forgiveness and the country's pride in its perseverance.

On another day, the team, Bahati, and I were on a bus headed to a school. We were going to spend a few hours practicing English with other students. Bahati was excited, because ever since we'd first connected, he'd continually tried to form full sentences in English when speaking to me. He would get shy and embarrassed when he saw the look of amusement on my face. I would encourage him to keep going, but eventually he would give up when the right words wouldn't come to him fast enough, and he would laugh it all off.

As the bus continued to make its way to our destination, I looked out the window and saw one of the most beautiful sights I had ever seen—endless fields of tall sunflowers reaching for the sun and extending toward the rolling hills. The cerulean background of the sky and the way the sun shone brightly above the sunflower fields made it hard to believe that only eighteen years before, this land had been the setting of some of Rwanda's darkest moments. That particular day, though, it absolutely took my breath away.

I murmured something about how much I love sunflowers and how beautiful the scene was. Bahati leaned in and pointed in the direction of the fields. "Mama, we hide," he said. It took me a while and the help of the translator to understand that he was referring to his memory of a time when he and a bunch of children ran and hid within the sunflowers in the darkness of night to escape the murderers. Later, I would hear similar stories from other survivors. I have never been able to look at a sunflower or a field of sunflowers the same way again. If anything, I am more grateful for their beauty and existence, and every time I see one, I say a prayer of thanks for their protection and abundance in Rwanda.

After returning to the United States, I spent the next few months in a state of depression. I was constantly irritated by how we as a society lived in excess and how we seemingly took for granted just how good we had it. It didn't help that a few days after I stepped off the plane from Rwanda, I was back on a plane to Las Vegas for a work conference. The stark differences between the quiet and serene landscape of Rwanda and the bustling noise and showiness of the Las Vegas Strip was jarring to all of my senses. I spent those next four days in and out of general sessions, sleeping in between trainings, and skipping out on all the touristy activities my colleagues were out there enjoying. It was my first time in Las Vegas, but all I saw were the four walls of the meeting spaces and the inside of my hotel room, and I was noticeably absent from all the team photos that documented this epic weekend the company had offered us.

I couldn't comprehend what I was feeling. Even though I hadn't seen my friends in months and was surrounded by them with the opportunity to have some fun, I couldn't let loose and enjoy myself. I was exhausted—emotionally and physically spent, still processing all that I had witnessed over the last few weeks. I would come to learn later that what I was experiencing were some of the stages of grief: denial, depression, even anger. Reacclimating to my normal life and life in our privileged Western world in general was difficult. When our mission team finally had the chance to gather and debrief, it was a week later. By then, I realized that it wasn't my friends and family who had changed. It was me.

I had changed.

Weeks went by, and I became restless again. I never felt satisfied. I needed to find something that I could do that would help me feel like my time in Rwanda had not been spent in vain. Since 2012 I've had a handful of "side hustles." One time I took on a full-time job for a few years to help contribute to our family income. After that, and with the increasing demand of my children's school and extracurricular schedules, I scaled back to part-time, but every job or side gig I ever took on was with all of my kids'—including Bahati's—future in mind. If something was tied to Africa in any way, I was drawn to do my part—some part—so in my own way I felt like I was still helping, creating positive changes for this place that had become a part of my being and an even bigger part of my heart and soul.

At our debriefing, I learned that typically people who opt to go on mission trips visit that country just once in their lives. For many, Africa would be a once-in-a-lifetime experience, and although the sponsorship commitment and relationship may continue and grow for years and years, many do not return for a myriad of reasons. I guess because Bahati's situation was different, and in our eyes dire, I always knew I would have to return. At the time, I didn't know how soon or exactly when, but I knew I would.

I threw myself into work and planned my next visit. I decided early on that I would return to Rwanda and that whatever I had to do to make that happen, I was willing to do. I spent the months before my next visit advocating for sponsorships. I asked my friends and family members to consider sponsoring a child. I promised them that when I returned to Rwanda, I would personally visit each of their children and bring them gifts and letters of hope and encouragement. I sold hand-carved wooden worry crosses made by Chris's aunt and donated the proceeds to my fundraising efforts. These pocket-sized crosses were something tangible one could hold in the palm of their hand as a reminder of God's love. I talked to anyone and everyone who would lend me an ear and listen to my Rwandan experiences. Eventually, with generous gifts from loved ones and the sales of those worry crosses, I raised enough funds to return to Rwanda less than a year later.

It was amazing to witness how much our son had grown in that short time. Bahati's English had vastly improved. His teachers and his house mom praised his efforts in school, and he was well liked by his peers. He had put on some much-needed weight, and he looked positively wonderful. It was clear to see how sponsorship had turned his life around. From the very beginning, Bahati had had a joyful soul, but his eyes had reflected how much suffering and sadness he had borne in his young life. Seeing how truly happy he was and noticing how his eyes sparkled when he recounted all the new and exciting things he had experienced over the course of the year made my mama heart swell with love and pride. He was growing physically, mentally, emotionally, and above all, faithfully. He was thriving. His love and unwavering faith in God was inspiring to us all. He told us how he had been invited to join the music ministry, lending his vocals and sometimes his drumming skills. He asked if I could bring him a guitar of his own the next time I visited, and I promised him I would. It would take a few more years, but we eventually got that guitar to him, and he took to it as if he had been playing his whole life. That guitar has naturally become an extension of our son. He is rarely seen without it strapped to his body.

Today, eight years later, Bahati is a grown man still living, studying, and working in Rwanda. He is a husband to his wife, Lethy, and father to their one-year-old son (our first grandbaby), Brian. Though time and distance separate us, we've continued to nurture a close relationship with them, thanks to the wonders of modern technology. Chris and I live for the day that we can be with them to hold our grandson for the first time and hug our son and daughter-in-love. Bahati can finally meet his dad and siblings. Through the years our children have witnessed how sponsorship, writing letters, and making connections abroad have made a positive impact not just for one person but also in their own lives. They've come to learn that by the simple act of loving one another, they can change the trajectory of another human being's life for the better.

I will always be a missionary at heart. Since June 19, 2012—that fateful day I first stepped foot on that rich, red African soil 7,545 miles away from home—I have nurtured this big, crazy, God-sized dream in my heart. One day I want to take small groups of women with me back to Rwanda. I want to help open their hearts and eyes to another level of compassion not only for those whose lives they would inevitably touch but for themselves too.

And why stop there? If I'm dreaming, I'm dreaming *big*. I envision offering guided mission trips to the Philippines, Uganda, Guatemala, and perhaps Turkey, in addition to Rwanda. Those countries are especially near and dear to me because I have strong familial ties to them. Having visited all but Turkey so far, I know there are many opportunities to serve. The need for those willing to spread love and hope is great all over the world.

Now, you might be thinking at this very minute that you can't do any of that. Maybe you're telling yourself the same lies I told myself all those years ago: *I don't have anything to offer. . . . I can't make a real difference, so why bother? . . . I'm just a mom, just a this or just a that. . . .* Perhaps you're feeling like you still aren't enough. Lies. All lies. In the words of Glinda the Good Witch from *The Wizard of Oz,* "You had the power all along, my dear." You are already equipped for this work because you are you. You were born with the innate gift to love and serve, whether you realize it or not. The beautiful thing is you do not have to go far or overseas to serve. The African continent or any of the countries I mentioned may not specifically speak to your heart, and that's okay. Until I went to Rwanda, Africa didn't speak to mine either. It took years and a simple invitation from a virtual stranger to plant that seed in my heart. Your path and your experiences will not necessarily look like mine, because we are each called to serve in different ways. Rest assured, we each have a purpose and an important role to play in this lifetime. You can still be a source of hope and a light to those in need, if only in your own backyard.

In 2018 I created a short-lived blog titled *Muster Joy.* Taking inspiration from a quote by Emily Dickinson that says, "The mere sense of living is joy enough" and because my word for that year was *joy*, my goal for the blog was to remind myself and others that joy can be found daily, even in the most mundane of tasks. Joy can be manifested anywhere; we just have to look for it. That blog no longer exists, but I dubbed myself Joymusterer, a completely made-up title I created to describe what I strive to be always—someone who can muster joy anytime and anywhere. I've had that handle for a few years now, and it has stuck. I am taking it full circle in wanting to make these trips abroad to help women find their joy.

I am calling these experiential trips Joy Journeys, because I want to help women like you and me discover the root of true joy—which I have come to appreciate is found only in the service of others and most certainly not in worldly things like material wealth or titles.

Yes, it's true—first and foremost *I'm just a mom*. That phrase no longer evokes guilt, shame, or feelings of being less than for me but instead fills me with overwhelming pride and satisfaction. Being a mom is the best role and calling I will ever have. It is a vocation I was called to serve, and until my African experience, I didn't understand or appreciate fully the magnitude of it all. I am *just a mom*, but I am much more than that too. I learned I don't need a fancy degree or a special skill set to make a difference in the world. I can leave an indelible imprint just by putting one foot in front of the other, by showing up. Who I am and what I have to offer is more than enough. Just like who you are and what you have to offer is more than enough. You are a gift, and what makes you *uniquely* you can be used to muster joy and serve others because you are "fearfully and wonderfully made" (Psalm 139:14).

To some, sponsorship may seem like it's just about charitable giving, but it truly goes deeper than that. It's about loving another human being and showing that person that he or she is worthy. It's about sharing God's love for them through acts of compassion. Plain and simple—it's about love.

I've been asked before, *"What did you do in Rwanda?"*

"Were you there on a medical mission?"

"Did you help build a new church?"

"Why would you want to go back again?"

Well, I'm not a doctor or a nurse, and I don't know the first thing about building anything, let alone a church, but I am a mom . . . a wife, a daughter, a sister, and a friend . . . and above all, I know how to love.

When my time is up and I leave this earth, the only thing I want to be remembered for is that I loved well.

Just a mom who loved well. That will be my legacy.

ABOUT THE AUTHOR

TESSA KIDD

As a navy brat and third-culture kid, Tessa Kidd has traveled extensively, only to discover that home is wherever her people are. Always with a notebook and pen in hand, she is convinced that we could change the world if everyone took up a daily habit of journaling.

Having labeled herself "just a mom," it took a heart-wrenching mission trip to Rwanda for Tessa to realize that being a mom equipped her to serve in the best possible way.

When she's not scribbling, or lost in a book, you can find her sipping her favorite Ugandan roast and sharing on her blog or Instagram about the people, places, and things that help her muster joy. Tessa believes her home is her sanctuary, love is her legacy, and true joy is found only in serving others.

For inspiration on ways to muster joy, visit Tessa's blog at tessakidd.com

Chapter 13

BUILD YOUR CONFIDENCE

Sheryl Morley

"By believing in yourself, you come to appreciate your worth, your purpose, and the result you want."

Challenge

The feeling of never fitting in, being embarrassed all the time, and lacking self-confidence was crushing my soul. I lived the first twenty-five years of my life not wanting to be me. I felt so inadequate. I wanted to escape, but I did not know how.

I was born on a chicken farm. My dad was an egg route driver. Outside was my heaven. I loved to ride my bike, play in the sandbox, and see the baby chicks when they arrived at the farm. Life took a disturbing turn when I had to start school. I did not want to be there. Everything I loved in life was taken away. I was made to sit, be quiet, and do as I was told. Everything was dark, boring, and hard. I could not focus. Learning to read was out of the question, and comprehending was even harder.

This continued for years. The teachers told my mom that I had a number of learning disabilities. I remember my mom telling me she felt like a total failure. I wasn't like anyone else. I was not as good as them, I was not as smart as them, and I would spend the next twenty years trying to be like them.

Instead of looking on the inside for qualities I had, I would always look outward. I always wanted to be someone else. I never felt good enough being me. Day after day, I wished I could become someone else, like Cinderella before the ball. To me, many other girls seemed to be exquisite examples of feminine beauty. Next to them, I thought I would forever be the ugly duckling.

Corky had the best hairstyle ever. I spent hours trying to make my hair appear just like hers. One morning I finally perfected the style. I knew for sure everyone would love my hair. I went to school that morning feeling amazing. *This is the day that things will be different*, I thought.

As I walked into school with pep in my step, everything went into slow motion. All the kids were standing around chatting, waiting for the morning bell to ring. I heard a number of girls compliment Corky: "You look so wonderful, Corky," and on and on. I was excited, because I knew they would come to me next. I knew that for the first time ever, my peers would tell me just how great I looked. Just then, a good friend of mine turned to me and said, "Sheryl, what did you do to your hair? Wait: did you curl it and then not comb it? That really doesn't look very good." Every single person standing there stared at me and then started laughing. I was humiliated. I had tried so hard. I wanted to be like Corky, but I was not Corky. I was just me after all, and it made me so depressed.

Another girl I spent hours trying to be like was Debra. She was beautiful, sweet, funny, and kind. She was everything I was not. Everyone loved Debra. I could just never measure up to her. Then there was Tiffany, a great friend. She had just moved to our small town from California. She was bigger than life and the best dancer ever! I really wanted to dance like her, so I had this great idea to try out for the high school drill team. Tryouts were in teams of two, and Tiffany really wanted me to be her partner. No one thought that was a good idea, since Tiffany had been taking dance lessons her whole life and the only dancing I had done was on the farm.

The day came for tryouts. I was beyond nervous and excited. But I knew, and had been told many times, that *everyone* makes the drill team. What did I have to lose? Tiffany and I tried out together. I thought it went great. I was sure I had made the team. A few days later, the names of the final team members were posted on the wall in the gym. Pages and pages of names. One hundred girls had made the team, with two alternates. The doors of the gym were opened. A hundred and three girls ran into the gym, screaming, laughing, and hoping to see their names on the wall. I watched as girls squealed and hugged each other when they found their names.

I moved closer to the wall and looked eagerly for my name. As more time went by without my seeing it, my excitement turned to fear. All my friends joined the search for my name. All of them had already found their names, and Tiffany had even been made one of the captains. I tried to be happy for them, but my greatest fear was starting to set in. As I searched harder and harder, the negative self-talk started. *You are so stupid. Why do you even try? You fail every time. You are such an idiot. There is not one thing in the world that you are good at.* I looked at every single name over and over again, all 102 of them. Maybe they had accidentally omitted my name, but no, maybe they had decided, once again, that Sheryl Morley was not good enough.

I felt a welling sense of hopelessness. I felt sick inside. All of my friends were eager to find my name, but finally I knew my name was not on the list, that it had intentionally been omitted. Everybody started saying, "Oh, I'm so sorry." Well, yeah, 102 people made it out of 103. I was the one person who did not make it. I just ran. I ran to the car, my mind screaming, *It's going to be all right. I will get over it. I'm fine, really. I'm fine, I'm fine.*

To make matters even worse, the only reason I had tried out for the drill team was that I didn't have enough self-confidence to try out for cheerleading. My self-confidence had now plummeted to an all-time low.

Change

I continued being "fine" until I was twenty-four, when by chance my mom gave me an audiotape of a health lecture by Dr. Joel Wallach. I did not want to listen to it, but after my mom repeatedly asked whether I had, I finally broke down and listened. It turned out to be the most interesting lecture on health I had ever heard. I began following Dr. Wallach's protocol, using products from a company that Dr. Wallach had partnered with, and my health improved dramatically. I lost all the weight I had gained, I got off prescription pain medication, and I began my journey of health. Within months I felt like a new person.

My mom knew the guy who had helped produce the health lecture recording. His name was Terry Porter, and he had a job opening for a representative to take orders over the phone for Dr. Wallach's health products. I really didn't want to take the job; my heart was set on being a cocktail waitress. This job opening required me to sell. I had done that before, and I was not doing it again. However, when I met with Terry, he told me the job was not about selling, but about sharing my story with people over the phone. I had a great story about how Dr. Wallach's program had helped me, so I decided to give it a try. I had been employed in several different jobs, and all of them had ended in failure. By the time I was twenty-five, more than thirty jobs hadn't worked out for me, but I always had hope that the next job would be the one.

I moved from Phoenix to Idaho and started working at
Terry Porter's office. When people called about an ad they
had seen, I would simply engage in a conversation with
them and share my health story. It worked like a charm! I
became the best on the phone team and had finally found
something I was really good at. Soon thereafter I actually
got to meet Dr. Wallach at Terry's office. He was not like
anyone I had ever met before. He was on a mission. He was
focused, driven, and living life on purpose. The movement
he had created with his audiotape was already legendary,
and he asked me to be his assistant and help him with his
live lecture tour. I decided to take the job.

I experienced amazing things on the road with Dr. Wallach.
I witnessed people's physical, emotional, and financial
health change dramatically because of his teachings,
vision, and commitment. After I toured with Dr. Wallach,
he decided to start his own company in January 1997. He
offered me a choice: work as a corporate employee for
his new company or build a team. The corporate position
was a guaranteed job paying an outrageous $10 per hour,
so I was definitely leaning in that direction. That was the
highest-paying job offer I had ever had, and I could not
even imagine making that much money. However, I have
always felt that my purpose in life is to contribute to other
people's lives in a significant way. When Dr. Wallach asked
me a few days later, I told him I had decided to build a
team. He was proud of my choice and told me he believed
in me and would mentor me.

For the first time in my life, someone believed in me. I was amazed that someone could see potential in me and believed I could have an impact on the world. I had always doubted myself. In the past, I hadn't even been able to make the team, and now I was supposed to build my *own* team? I had a small glimmer of hope. I thought that with Dr. Wallach's mentorship, maybe, just maybe, I could make this work. Before long, something shocking happened. Through clarity, consistency, and courage I began to build an enormous team. Dr. Wallach's vision became my vision and is still my vision now, twenty-six years later.

For five years I traveled with Dr. Wallach, building my business. Several horrific events happened when he and I were on the road. For example, all the products, computers, and bags were stolen out of our van. We stayed at a hotel with a meth lab that underwent a police bust while we were there. But no matter what was going on in the world, Doc convinced me that the show must go on. We did a seminar every night in a different town 340 days a year. Doc said the mission and vision always take precedence. There are people out there who need us, he said.

I was part of something bigger than myself for the first time in my life, and it felt fabulous. Being on the road every single day, setting up the seminar, processing orders, answering questions, and helping people on their health journey caused my self-confidence to grow. A weakness I had had my whole life was becoming a strength. Determination, drive, and discipline were and are the core values Dr. Wallach lives by (and spent every day for years teaching me I had to live by). He made me realize there is much more to life—that there are more opportunities and things out there that I can do and ways that I can help people.

Celebration

Having Dr. Wallach as a mentor completely changed my life. I went from feeling that I never fit in anywhere to a sense that I belonged to something bigger than myself. Looking back, I see that Dr. Wallach didn't fit in anywhere either. Instead of trying to fit in, he decided to build his own tribe. He taught me how to do the same. Now I have my own tribe and more loving connections than I could ever have imagined. In the end, fitting in was all about following. I now knew that I did not have to fit in, because I could blaze my own trails. Rather than fit in, I could stand out. I did not have to be like people who were popular. I could derive all the satisfaction in the world from helping others become better in mind, body, and spirit.

I had always just gotten through life any way I could, always very unsure of myself, unsure what would happen next, and unsure which direction I should go. Dr. Wallach helped me clarify all of these things, allowing me to achieve success and freedom. I really had to get to a place where what I thought of myself was more important than what others thought of me. I went from feeling embarrassed all the time to feeling good in my own skin. Dr. Wallach helped me do that.

Dr. Wallach was absolutely certain about his mission, and he didn't care what other people thought. It was more important to get the message of health and wellness out than what the doubters and naysayers said or thought. No distraction could take him off course, because he had such clarity of purpose about the result he wanted. I learned that it is essential to be absolutely certain of the direction you want to go in life and to never give up. Knowing that there are people out there who need us and that it's a matter of life and death pushed Dr. Wallach through every adversity he faced. Being a part of his unrelenting quest to save people's health changed the way I felt and the way I lived.

My lack of consistency in every area of my life used to cause me to doubt myself. Consistency builds self-confidence. The consistency of being on the road every day, talking to thousands of people, and helping them on their health journeys made me begin to trust myself. Self-confidence is one of the greatest gifts I received from having Dr. Wallach as my mentor. I started feeling better about myself because he helped me realize all the fabulous qualities I already had. I discovered that I had drive, determination, and the discipline needed to become extremely successful.

I sometimes pause to think about what my life would be like if I didn't have Dr. Wallach as a mentor. I feel that if I had turned down that opportunity and chosen not to make that crucial pivot, I would still be in the same downward spiral I was in when I met him. I realized on this journey that life does not unfold before you; it is what you make of it. If I hadn't gone through all the struggles, hard times, and painful experiences, I would not have been able to last one week with Dr. Wallach.

Before I worked for Dr. Wallach, he fired thirty women in thirty days. The strength I gained in my younger years toughened me enough to do what needed to be done. Dr. Wallach saw qualities in me that I couldn't see in myself, and because he believed in me so much and kept believing in me, I started believing in me too. Maybe I could do it after all. Maybe I was good enough. Maybe I did have great skills. Maybe I did have a purpose in life.

Another thing Dr. Wallach encouraged me to do was make a vision board. I was so opposed to making a vision board. I was afraid to wish for something and not have it happen. I then purposely put things on my vision board that I knew had no chance of happening. I thought that was a way to avoid coping with my fear. I am here to tell you that every single thing I thought would never happen that I put on the vision board has in fact happened. I have an amazing husband, two wonderful kids, the home of my dreams, time, and financial freedom. Because I followed my heart and chose to follow Dr. Wallach, my life is absolutely fabulous.

Dr. Wallach gave me the greatest gift by being my mentor. I have now made it my life's mission to give the same gifts to others. Most super-successful people have a mentor who helped them. Tony Robbins always talks about Jim

Rohn. Jim Rohn always refers to Earl Shoaff. John Maxwell's two mentors were Robert Schuller and John Wooden, whom he followed and learned from daily.

I look at a mentor as a farmer. It reminds me of planting seeds back on the farm. You have to plant a seed, water a seed, and make sure weeds don't grow around the seed and strangle it. You have to nurture and protect the seed until it can stand on its own and bear fruit. In the beginning, every seed needs a mentor to help it get started on its journey from fine to fabulous.

Going from fine to fabulous is a process. When I was "just fine," I was always pretending everything was okay. I was looking outside for validation and love instead of inside. I believed everyone was better than I was, and I could not see my talents and true potential. I felt overwhelmed, stressed, anxious, stupid, and hopeless. I believed there was no way out, that I was never good enough, and that I would never be successful. I didn't know what I wanted, I had no idea what my purpose in life was, and I was completely confused about how to take the first step out of my miserable condition.

Being fabulous means knowing that you are stronger than any problem you are facing. It means looking inside for clarity, love, joy, peace, validation, and courage. It means believing in yourself and your abilities, and that you were put here to have an impact on the world. It means feeling love, joy, peace, excitement, gratitude, success, and fulfillment. By believing in yourself, in your innate potential, you can accomplish anything, and no problem is too big for you to handle. By believing in yourself, you come to appreciate your worth, your purpose, and the result you want.

Don't wish it was easier, wish you were better. Don't wish for less problems, wish for more skills.
— Jim Rohn

ABOUT THE AUTHOR

SHERYL MORLEY

Sheryl Morley began her career in direct sales in 1997, when she joined Dr. Joel D. Wallach on a national tour to promote his new company, Youngevity International. She recommends his nutritional formulations for health and wellness. Sheryl has been the master distributor at Youngevity since 1997. She has an organization of more than 300,000 people and does more than $10 million per month in sales. In 2018 Sheryl was inducted into the Network Marketing Pro Million Dollar Hall of Fame, and she has achieved Youngevity's highest rank of Black Diamond Ambassador. Sheryl's passion is to promote optimal wellness through nutritional supplementation and healthy lifestyle choices. She is also the co-founder of the Institute of Wholistic Health, which trains and certifies health coaches. She finds joy in teaching women how to achieve financial independence and time freedom.

Sheryl is married to Jonathan Emord, is the mother of twins, a boy and a girl. In 2017, she was named Mother of the Year in the Washington metropolitan area by *Washington FAMILY* magazine. She teaches multiple classes per week in the areas of mindset, leadership, and weight loss.

You can learn more about Sheryl at www.SherylMorley.com

Chapter 14

GROW YOUR FAITH

Penny Pereboom

"I accepted my brokenness as part of God's plan to grow me into the woman I was to become."

Early in my marriage, I decided it was not my husband's job to make me happy. After all, he had bigger fish to fry and a very stressful job as a navy pilot, defending our country. I wanted to be an obedient wife and an excellent mother, and I decided I would have to figure out a way to be happy on my own. I proceeded to fill every spare moment of my time with kids' activities, volunteering, hobbies, graduate school, and working as a teacher. After I'd spent seventeen years as a navy spouse, my husband retired and the kids left home, but I still filled my time with the house, hobbies, volunteering, the yard, work, and more work. I was really looking forward to an end to all the military deployments, but we decided my husband would accept a job as a contractor and continue to fly for the military in Afghanistan. The job meant he would deploy for a month at a time, every other month. Hence, the reason I kept busy. I was miserable otherwise.

When does the happily-ever-after start? We'd put in all the work. We'd scrimped and saved and invested. We'd made it from survival mode to security to success. For my husband, that was the pinnacle of his life. He was successful and content. As for me, I wanted to feel significant by providing value to others, and I wanted him to be on that journey with me. I went on a relentless pursuit to have it all until my life took an unexpected turn. I lost my husband, my dream home, a good chunk of my thriving real estate business, and a lot of my friends. Before this unfolded, though, I was already alone. I found myself inside an empty house with my husband away yet again, this time by his choice, even though he had other options available that would have allowed him to be home, building a future with me.

Before the unraveling took place, I was a top-producing real estate agent with some very big goals being powered by a "big Why" to bring my husband home from Afghanistan for good. Seventeen years as a navy wife had included enough deployments to last a lifetime. Now that my husband had retired from the military, I wanted him home. I wanted to enjoy barbecues with friends, get involved in our community, take vacations, and celebrate holidays surrounded by family and friends. Living in my dream home alone half the year was not ideal, yet I endured it so my husband could continue to pursue his dream of flying military operations.

Alone. I would sit alone on the patio surrounding the pool, feeling as if I was at some sort of Texas Hill Country resort. The landscaping was breathtaking. The veranda expansion, the balcony reconstruction, the addition of a staircase, and the fresh sod coupled with native plants were well worth the several thousand dollars we'd spent. Only it wasn't a resort. It was our dream home, and a far cry from the military housing where we had lived for most of the time we were married. I remember looking at the empty wicker chair next to me and recalling my grandmother sitting there, crocheting away, glancing up from her current project only briefly to say sternly, "You could have had a third of this and given the rest to the poor." Oh, how those words still linger in my head whenever I am encouraged to dream bigger, treat myself, or indulge in anything lavish or unnecessary. She had a good point. Did I really need all of this? Were all the sacrifices I had made for seventeen years as a navy wife worth having this now, with nobody to share it with? Was I living in accordance with God's will?

My loneliness, coupled with my need to feel significant, motivated me to put a plan into action. My grandmother's comment was especially piercing because she had such a strong faith in God. It left me feeling as if I was not serving Him well. The way I understood God at the time was that He was someone whose grace and mercy I had to earn. With an abundance of blessings came an overwhelming obligation to glorify God and obey His Word. After spending countless hours reading motivational books, partaking in Bible studies, attending invigorating seminars, and contemplating the plan for my future, I wrote a new mission statement for my personal life and my business, replacing my previous big Why with "To use the blessings that God has so richly blessed me with to bless others." I made it my mission to empower people to connect their inner purpose and passion with outer goals and strategies to bring about extraordinary and sustainable results. I became obsessed with growing myself and subsequently growing my income and then using it to bless the world. That was my answer! How could I be unhappy if I made it my life's mission to bless the world? How could I not be pleasing to God when I was sharing the gifts that He blessed me with? How could I not make a significant impact in the lives of those around me? Confident, clear, and connected with my vision, I set my plan into action with unbridled enthusiasm and delight.

Until this point in my life I had not had the mental or physical capacity to disengage from the obligations of motherhood to embark on something that would take my focus and attention away from my children. Now that the kids were independent, I could give my energy to other endeavors. Ready to blow the lid off my bottled-up ambition, I found new and exciting opportunities to engage my mind, serve God, and find significance in my work. I was no longer tethered to attending to my children's needs. I was not leaving them behind at all, but I was leaving behind motherhood as I had known it. As I started heading down this path toward significance, I became keenly aware that I was going to have to leave some people behind.

As I grew professionally, emotionally, and spiritually, I realized I was leaving my spouse behind, too. He had his own mission, and it was not congruent with mine. We went about our lives, respecting each other's wants and needs, living quite amicably and simply taking care of business, much like roommates. We were passionate, just not passionate about each other. I thought that this was how people stayed in good marriages forever. They simply led separate fulfilling lives, together. I did not feel loved, respected, or appreciated, but every time I lamented about it, I reminded myself of the commitment I had made nearly twenty-two years earlier when I got married. I was convinced that the enemy (otherwise known as Satan) was wedging his way into my perfect life, trying to destroy me and thereby shattering my faith in God. Fear, doubt, and worry are the enemy's tactics. The enemy has a conniving and shrewd way of concocting a plan to bring me to my knees.

No, Satan! Not today. I will remain faithful and loving to my spouse, even if I don't feel he loves, respects, or appreciates me. I needed God's help, but I did not know how to seek it at the time. Instead, I took matters into my own hands. I knew exactly what I needed to do to fight Satan, or so I thought. Unfortunately, I fell right into his trap.

Fall is the time of year when I can finally take a breath after the busy real estate season. The cool, refreshing air lures me back into the yard in preparation for a glorious spring ahead. I prune bushes, extract weeds, and dig in the dirt with a glee that no normal person has for yard work. An acre and a half of beautiful Texas Hill Country doesn't come without excruciating work. When I was working in the yard, I was no longer brooding or lamenting the choice we had made for my husband to take a job that took him away to Afghanistan for half the year. Blessed with a very flexible work schedule, I would spend hours in the yard. I didn't know the toll it was taking on my body, especially my hip, until I crawled out of bed one day after a full workout in the yard. Compounded over time, the yard benefited far more than my body.

The arduous task of creating a Hill Country resort in my backyard would not only occupy my mind so I wasn't brooding but, I was convinced, also please my husband. What made me think this was the way to his heart? I had relentlessly worked on our landscaping, remodeled the house, and built a thriving real estate business, all to win his affection, respect, and appreciation. Clearly it was not working. I knew my spouse would be much more receptive to my spicing things up in the bedroom, and I would say I was successful in that department. We were having some of the best intimate moments ever in our marriage until the day it all came to a screeching halt.

My spouse was not very talkative, and it was difficult to get him to share with me what he needed until the fateful day I remember so clearly. We were drinking wine on our front porch. I was admiring the landscaping and planning the next twelve projects. He was surely dreading all the work and the honey-do list I greeted him with at the airport every time he came home from his latest trip overseas. That day, I was finally successful in getting him to talk openly about what he really wanted in our relationship. The details are not nearly as important as how the words he uttered made me feel. He did not have to say the exact words for it to become evident that I was not enough for him. He couldn't have cared less about the yard, the house, or the increase in income. He wanted something I could never give him. The words he spoke, the unfulfilled desires he expressed, and the lack of regard for my feelings created a tremendous ache in my heart that compounded over the next few years. My sorrow was unbearable, and as I retold the story to my friends, the tears started flowing almost daily. I felt unappreciated, disrespected, and unloved. Nevertheless, I pulled myself together, and with the same determination I had for the yard and my career, I proceeded to work on pruning, fertilizing, and extracting weeds from our marriage.

The yearning in my heart for a loving relationship with my husband grew, and the pain in my hip from years of laboring in the yard and trying to make my home the perfect oasis became unbearable. The physical strain was more than I could endure and finally led to the dreadful prognosis. . . . Hip replacement surgery was imminent. If only surgery and physical therapy could replace the broken parts in our marriage. How great would it be if I could trade in my bruised heart for a brand-new one. The bum hip didn't help matters, since I couldn't exercise and gained weight. Eventually I weighed nearly fifty pounds more than I weighed the day we promised to love each other for better or worse. I sought comfort from my husband and friends, but no one could mend my feelings of unworthiness and unattractiveness.

It was not for lack of trying. My husband supported my business endeavors, planned a beautiful vacation to Greece for our twenty-fifth wedding anniversary, enabled me to create our Hill Country resort, and helped me host elaborate family celebrations. He could not fathom why that was not enough for me, just like I could not accept the fact that I was not enough for him. I wanted him home, and I felt he enjoyed his time away from home just a little too much. The rift kept widening.

I continued to toil in the yard even though my hip continued to deteriorate. I worked countless hours on my real estate career, and in my spare time I worked on my professional coaching certification. My search for significance continued as I found ways to win the affection, respect, and appreciation of colleagues and clients so I could regain some feeling of worthiness. My spouse and I continued to grow apart. I had been successful in building a very successful real estate career, which allowed him to quit working in Afghanistan, only for him to take another job where he was gone for a month at a time to Colombia. I wanted him to live his dream, but it was a huge strain on our marriage. I asked myself why he insisted on being away from me. Why couldn't he work closer to home? We were not desperate for that income. I was desperate for his affection, and I grew increasingly bitter and cold.

I kept as busy as I could so I would not face the unhappiness I was feeling. I had so much to be thankful for, and whenever I was depressed or lonely, I felt as though I was being ungrateful, selfish, and shallow. I reached out to friends who, suffice it to say, are no longer my friends. It wasn't that we merely lost touch. No. They told me they did not want to be my friend anymore but would not share with me why. It was extremely hurtful. It became apparent that I was going to have to leave them behind in pursuit of a very demanding career and some very lofty goals. My ambition and determination did not sit well with girlfriends who wanted to wine, dine, and shop during working hours, especially when my working hours went well into the evening and weekend. I proceeded to fill my world with like-minded friends, but it still made my heart ache to lose the ones I'd once had. Oh, how the enemy loved to fill my head with what hurt instead of all the blessings I had in my life. All I could focus on was what I lacked. Needless to say, I was no fun to be around.

The enemy knows how much relationships mean to me, and I am convinced he put thoughts in my head about this experience to exacerbate my despondent emotional state. Even though I worked relentlessly to have a beautiful home, a thriving yard, a successful career, a deeper relationship with God, and a loving marriage, I was failing miserably at the things that mattered to me most: my spouse, my friends, and my family. No amount of home improvement or self-improvement could distract me from my sadness anymore. I was crying all the time, much to the dismay of my husband, who was unable to ease my hurt. If only he'd been able to see that all I needed was for him to show me love, respect, and appreciation. I desperately needed a friend, and instead I just kept pushing him, my family, and my friends further and further away. As much as people care about me, they are simply ill equipped to understand my pain when all they can see are the blessings I have around me. How could I be so upset? Only God could understand. He knows my heart and is always there for me. I comprehended this concept, but I didn't do a very good job of seeking God's consoling. I continued to whine to the people around me until I became unbearable to be with.

My intuition started sounding the alarm. *He's cheating on you. He must be. Look at you. You're fat. You're unattractive. You're physically weak. Your health continues to decline. And all you talk about is work . . . working in the yard, working on your business, working on strengthening your relationship with God. After spending seventeen years working on raising your kids—alone most of the time—you're ready to reap the rewards of your sacrifices, and no one is around to do that with because you have whined your way out of those relationships. Your gorgeous home and prosperous career are worthless. You are worthless. The work you do is insignificant. Your goal to bless others is unattainable because you are a miserable soul. They see you with all your blessings and they despise you. Your mind is whirling around with so much self-doubt that you will never accomplish anything. You will never be able to live in accordance with God's will. You cannot even commit to studying God's Word.*

There was a battle going on in my mind. The enemy was attacking me. He knew exactly how to bring me down, for he had been strategizing the war in my head since the very beginning of my marriage (and probably even long before then). As my husband and I grew further apart, the enemy wedged his way into our lives. His favorite tactic is to destroy us and take everything away from us to prove to God that we will no longer follow Him when we are distraught, discouraged, and disappointed.

My prayers were answered when I learned about the weapons made available to me since birth that guaranteed victory. The weapons at my disposal would enable me to fight the demons of depression, loneliness, anxiety, insecurity, unworthiness, and guilt. The weapons I am referring to are God's Word, worship, and prayer. I prayed for peace and enlightenment. I made it part of my business and personal plan to strengthen my relationship with God. This became my primary goal when I realized, after my grandmother with her piercing glance reminded me, that I was clearly neglecting God's calling and instead, pursuing what my ego longed for . . . the house, the spouse, the friends, the vacations, the family gatherings, the wealth, the success, and the continued abundance that I was already enjoying. It's not that pursuing these things is bad. There is no doubt that God wants us to be fruitful, prosperous, and blessed. It was the way in which I was pursuing my lofty goals as a means to find purpose and value in the world that had caused me to veer off course and into the pit I now found myself in.

Let me reiterate. God wants us to live a beautiful, abundant life, full of blessings, love, and joy. The problem comes when we are deceived by the enemy just as Eve was deceived in the Garden of Eden. The enemy had taken my thoughts captive, and I was enslaved to meet the world's standards to feel good about myself. I had been deceived into believing that success would bring fulfillment and happiness. I had become addicted to the approval of others at a very young age. I had fallen into a performance trap, believing my worth was measured by my ability to exceed the standards and expectations set forth by my family, my teachers, my employers, my friends, and my spouse. I was a victim of self-condemnation and self-deprecation, feeling unworthy of love or even the blessings God had bestowed upon me and my family. Worst of all, I felt extreme shame when I failed to meet the standards, gain approval, and rise above self-condemnation. An abundant life was not the problem. The means by which I went about creating an abundant life was a huge detriment to my ability to enjoy it.

I continued to pray until God's message became loud and clear. I deployed the weapons at my disposal. I proceeded to learn God's Word as if I was in graduate school. I attended church and at least two Bible studies a week and added a Christian music playlist on my YouTube channel so I could sing His praises daily. I shared the wisdom I was gaining with others. I gave God the glory for all the good things that were happening in my life and all the blessings He continually bestowed on me.

Everything in my life was so very glorious! So why was I still crying all the time? As it turns out, the enemy saw an opening. He saw an opportunity to wreak havoc in my life, and even when I figured it out and turned to God, he did not relent. I battled with temptation, but little did I know, my husband was battling it as well. The enemy proceeded to bring him down and won that battle. My husband succumbed to temptation and had an affair, and subsequently my world turned upside down. In the months that followed I would lose the house, the spouse, a good chunk of my business, and several friends.

I went through the stages of grief one would expect. At first, I denied that this would end my marriage. We would get through this. Then I isolated myself from friends and family and cried endlessly. I documented my grief in prayers to God. My grief eventually turned into anger, which I expressed in some rather terse emails and texts to my husband. I wanted him to feel the hurt I was feeling. My Christian women friends kept telling me that God would restore my marriage, so I started to bargain with my husband, even telling him he could keep his mistress while we worked things out. In response to my pleas, he adamantly refused, which sent me into the depression that affected my health, my business, and my friendships. I cried every single day. My business declined. I grew increasingly weary and despondent.

As I started to accept my new reality, I sought solace in friends and spent time dining out, going to bars, and shopping . . . lots of shopping. I bought a new home and filled it with new furnishings. I started rebuilding my business and attending seminars again. Nevertheless, nothing brought back my joy.

How could it be that just a few short months earlier I had committed to growing my relationship with God, only to have my life as I knew it turned completely upside down? It was *not* what I had prayed for. I was ready to surrender. I continued to pray and immersed myself in learning God's Word. I did not surrender to the enemy. Instead, I surrendered to God's plan. I accepted my brokenness as part of God's plan to grow me into the woman I was to become. The enemy might have won this battle, but he had not won the war. I put on my armor and got ready to fight.

In God's playbook, which is how I affectionately refer to His Word, the penalties (otherwise known as sins) have consequences. God is the coach. Jesus and the Holy Spirit are the defensive and offensive coordinators. We think we know how to play the game better than the coach. We go about making decisions in the game of life without following the playbook or the coach's will. The coach is watching, shaking his head, because in his playbook he made the decision to give us free will. He created the plays and penalties, but we ultimately get to decide if and how to follow them.

The battle is ongoing, and I have to keep reminding myself that I have the weapon! I continually go back to God, and He is patiently waiting for me. He has prepared a table before me in the presence of my enemies: the mistress, the gossipers, the bad dates with men after my divorce, the thoughtless friends, the guilt-evoking family members, and Satan himself. God waits patiently at the table, and "I'm late for a very important date" as I dillydally with distractions and temptations. At God's table I get to partake in a feast! A feast of His wisdom, strength, and joy. A feast that He prepares for me to partake in *daily*. I leave the table with a cup spilling over with blessings.

My business is flourishing. I bought another home and kept my first one as an investment. I put in a beautiful new patio. I traveled to Hawaii with my daughter, where I spent time with some amazing friends. I have amazing business colleagues who are committed to helping me grow. I have met the most remarkable group of Christian women who know God's Word at an extremely high level and encourage me to do the same. I've rekindled friendships with my lifelong friends who did not desert me as I pursued my goals. My children are flourishing. Oh, the enemy constantly tries to convince me that I am unattractive, unworthy of love, and incapable of blessing others, and that God can't help me. I have found, nevertheless, that he does not come around when I am immersed in God's Word, worship, and praise. The great news is I can go back to God's table daily for all I can devour in terms of wisdom, strength, and joy. He's waiting.

I continue to gain courage and strength from God daily. I learned that the foundation of our marriage was so weak that no amount of rain or sunshine or nutrients could help. In our haste to start a family and buy our first home, in addition to deployments and military relocations, we had failed to establish a solid foundation built on God's love and promises. Focusing on Him I know I am deeply loved, I am wonderfully pleasing to Him, and He accepts me exactly as I am. There are no standards to meet, and there's no approval to gain. Oh, there are sins though. God put those in place to keep me from harm. Not all sins have immediate consequences, but they are nevertheless sins, because they tend to cause harm and dismay in the long run, either in our lives or in the lives of others. God knows I am going to sin, and He forgives me when I repent.

Armed with the wisdom I gain when I sit at God's table, following the example God gave us in Jesus, and being still and quiet so the Holy Spirit can guide me, I am able to recognize when I am being lured by the enemy toward my old, ingrained programming. Once I become aware of it, I can then eject detrimental thoughts that tend to produce negative results in my life. I am able, with the strength that comes from God when I worship Him and pray, to replace the faulty programming for a better outcome. It takes work, awareness, and most of all, surrender.

ABOUT THE AUTHOR

PENNY PEREBOOM

The firstborn of immigrant parents, Penny Pereboom inherited a strong entrepreneurial spirit and aimed to become a successful businesswoman. Nevertheless, she was also influenced by her traditional Greek Orthodox grandmother and suppressed her ambition while pursuing a fulfilling role as a successful homemaker.

Seventeen years as a navy wife and three children later, Penny popped the cork on her bottled-up ambition and became a top producing Texas real estate agent. With an extensive background in training and development and a master's degree in educational technology, she is on a mission to coach, train, and mentor others.

Divorce threw a wrench into her plans and nearly thwarted Penny's ambition, but from the depths of her despair she heard a distinct calling to tell the story of the wisdom, discernment, and joy she discovers daily in God's Word. He is equipping her to share his love, mercy, and grace with others.

Work With April

April Adams Pertuis is a visibility and media specialist with a career spanning more than 30 years in the television and video industry. She is an award-winning journalist who has worked for CBS Television, HGTV, DIY Network, and the Food Network.

Today April works with people and brands to help them tell their story in a more authentic way so they can transform their lives and businesses.

April's passion is working with women - equipping and empowering them to share their stories in bigger, bolder ways. She has helped thousands of women step on stages, write books, create podcasts, build ministries, and exponentially grow their business and impact.

To learn more about working with April, book a free call: www.lightbeamers.com/apply

About LIGHTbeamers

April Adams Pertuis' passion for storytelling and creating community with women led her to create LIGHTbeamers - a safe space to explore your story, find support, and get training on how to excavate the layers of your story to use in a positive, powerful way.

Using the weekly story prompts and private community, members have open and honest conversations about life, business, personal growth, and spirituality. It's a place to learn more about storytelling as it relates to your own life and business.

LIGHTbeamers also offers online courses, group coaching, and training programs, as well as high-level mentorship for women leaders who are ready to step into their brave and share their story with more people.

Members are CEOs, entrepreneurs, spiritual and civic leaders, change-makers, missionaries, teachers, and healers. They use their story every day to create community, effect change, and make a positive impact in the world by shining their light.

To learn more about the LIGHTbeamers community and suite of programs, go to www.lightbeamers.com

About the Inside Story Podcast

The Inside Story Podcast takes you behind the curtain of the biggest success stories of entrepreneurs, thought leaders, and change-makers.... people who have walked through fire and come out on the other side brighter. They aren't mechanical or scripted. They are unabashedly authentic and real. And they are generating massive success & fulfillment as a result!

The goal of the **Inside Story** is to inspire you to think about your own story, and learn to share it so it can shine a light for others.

Listen in to discover unique storytelling tips and mechanics that will empower you to tell your story in a whole new way. Learn more and listen at www.lightbeamers.com/podcast

About Our Pay-It-Forward Partnership

**100% of royalties from Amazon sales of this book will be directed to KIVA, with a special interest given to funding micro-loans to help women to start and grow businesses.**

Kiva is an international nonprofit, founded in 2005 in San Francisco, with a mission to expand financial access to help underserved communities thrive.

They do this by crowdfunding loans and unlocking capital for the underserved, improving the quality and cost of financial services, and addressing the underlying barriers to financial access. Through Kiva's work, students can pay for tuition, women can start businesses, farmers are able to invest in equipment and families can afford needed emergency care.

Learn more at www.kiva.org

Be In Our Next Book

Have you dreamt of becoming a published author but felt stuck and overwhelmed about where to even begin? If you are shaking your head yes, then this is for you.

The LIGHTbeamers *She Gets Published* Author Program is an opportunity to dip your toe into the world of writing and publishing without having to create an entire book or trying to figure things out in isolation.

Inside this 9-month group coaching program led by April Adams Pertuis (LIGHTbeamers) and Lanette Pottle (She Gets Published & Positivity Lady Press), you'll be guided every step of the way – from selecting and writing the right story, to creating your author platform, to marketing and selling your books.

You'll learn behind-the-scenes details of the publishing process as you work with a professional publisher and team of editors and book designers. PLUS the story you write inside the program will be published in the next release for the LIGHTbeamers collaborative book series – just like the women in this book.

Learn more and join the waitlist at www.lightbeamers.com/author